INTO THE SILENCE

A Biblical Perspective and Plan for Reaching the Deaf around the World

By

Joe Kotvas

Missionary to the Deaf
Lima, Peru - South America
www.efata.org   jkotvas@efata.org

Into the Silence
A Biblical Perspective and Plan for Reaching the Deaf Around the World

Copyright © 2006, 2018 by Joe Kotvas
2nd Edition

Joe Kotvas
1819 Hill Avenue
Ft. Myers, FL 33901
(813)675-4879
Jkotvas@efata.org

Published and printed by:
Faithful Life Publishers
North Fort Myers, FL 33903
(888) 720.0950
info@FaithfulLifePuyblishers.com

FaithfulLifePublishers.com

All Scripture quotations are from the King James Version of the Holy Bible.

All rights in this book are reserved. The material in this book may be freely copied as needed for use in ministry or for education purposes.

22 21 20 19 18   2 3 4 5 6

This book is dedicated to all those who have gone before in pioneering Deaf ministry in the United States as well as throughout the entire world. It is also dedicated to those who will follow in the future to reach the millions of deaf people who have yet to have the opportunity to understand the Gospel of the Lord Jesus Christ.

IN MEMORY OF WALLACE VERNON MILLER

PIONEERING DEAF MISSIONARY

DECEMBER 6, 1932 – NOVEMBER 14, 2006

Contents

Contents

And let the beauty of the LORD our God be upon us: and establish thou the work of our hands upon us; yea, the work of our hands establish thou it.
- Psalm 90:17

And in that day shall the deaf hear the words of the book, and the eyes of the blind shall see out of obscurity, and out of darkness.
- Isaiah 29:18

And were beyond measure astonished, saying, He hath done all things well: he maketh both the deaf to hear, and the dumb to speak.
- Mark 7:37

Then the eyes of the blind shall be opened, and the ears of the deaf shall be unstopped.
- Isaiah 35:5

A CHILD IS BORN,
A HEART TENDER AND DEAR.
A TREASURE THEY HAVE,
BUT ALAS, SHE CANNOT HEAR.

EYES SO BRIGHT,
A MIND EAGER TO LEARN.
BUT TO THEM "SHE'S A CANCER."
THEY WISH SHE'D NEVER BEEN BORN.

"WHY DIDN'T YOU ABORT HER?"
THE DOCTOR SIGHS.
"A CURSE SHE WILL BE,
FOR THE REST OF YOUR LIVES."

BUT HER MAKER LOVES HER.
PRECIOUS IS SHE.
IN HIS EYES SHE HAS VALUE.
A JEWEL SHE WILL BE.

HE LAY ON OUR HEARTS
A BURDEN SO GREAT.
FOR THESE LITTLE ONES
WHO "JUST DON'T RATE."

WITH A BURDEN TO SHARE
GOD'S GREAT LOVE THROUGH OUR HANDS,
SIGN LANGUAGE WE LEARNED
SO THEY'D UNDERSTAND.

A HOME, A CHURCH, A SCHOOL
AND HEARTS FULL OF LOVE;
DISCIPLINE AND WISDOM
FROM OUR FATHER ABOVE.

THIS CHILD IS NOW GROWING,
CAN READ AND CAN WRITE.
A "CANCER"? NO!
SHE'S PRECIOUS IN GOD'S SIGHT.

-LISA KOTVAS

(The quoted comments in this poem were actual comments made by parents of
our deaf children at *Efata*)

ACKNOWLEDGEMENTS

No work of this nature would be possible without the collaborative efforts and time of others. I would like to acknowledge the following people for their encouragement and help on this book.

- LISA – My dear wife and true "HELP MEET"♡

- Jon Barr, David Bennett, Manuel Caceres, Austin Gardner, Chris Gardner, Steve Houghton, Tony Howeth, John Olson, Shane Rice, Jim Sloan, and Arlene Van Horn.

All of the above had some part in the inspiration, preparation, direction, and editing of this book. They each took of their time to read this book and give me encouragement, constructive comments and critiques. ***THANK YOU*** to all of you for your help and encouragement to me for this project.

In every thing give thanks: for this is the will of God in Christ Jesus concerning you.   *- 1 Thessalonians 5:18*

Thanks be unto God for his unspeakable gift.
- 2 Corinthians 9:15

PREFACE

Into the Silence was written with the intent to motivate, challenge and educate God's servants regarding the needs and uniqueness of ministering among the Deaf. It is also intended to serve as an informative introductory text for Deaf ministry and missions for pastors and Christian servants alike.

There are many books on deafness, deaf education, sign language and Deaf culture. However, there are not many that deal with the subject of Deaf missions and the great need for missionaries and ministries for the Deaf worldwide.

This book is an effort to help fill that need and to provide motivation and vision to those who would give their lives to the Lord in the service of the Deaf.

Statistics presented have been researched but have not been scientifically verified. They were gleaned and developed from various sources with the intent of adding context to the need for ministry among the Deaf.

When referring to the use of the word *deaf* in this book, "**deaf**" is used in reference to the medical/audiological/pathological loss of hearing and "**Deaf**" is used as it relates to Deaf community and Deaf culture.

This book is primarily based on my personal experience, observation and opinion. *It is not intended to contradict, criticize or stand above another's opinions or methods of ministry.*

I pray you will find this book helpful and insightful; especially to those whom God has called to work with the Deaf or those who are considering a Deaf ministry in their church as part of their global missionary effort.

Time is short. We must be busy about the Master's business in reaching this greatly under-reached people group.

INTRODUCTION

In Peru, South America, it is a damp and overcast Sunday morning, as are most winter mornings in Lima. It's not too cool by North American standards, but for the average Peruvian, a bit more than they would like.

People continue to file into the church filling the pews. Men and women, boys and girls and even a few of "man's best friends" try to sneak in for the morning service.

The song leader beckons to begin the service by waving his hands to get the attention of the worshipers. He waves grandly and motions for all to stand. The service begins. There are no songbooks to hold. The words are projected onto a screen. You see, this is a Deaf church; they need their hands to sing!

A man is called to the platform to pray. He is deaf as well. He begins to pray and a voice interpreter interprets for the hearing people in the service. The man prays invoking God's blessing and help for the service in his language - Peruvian Sign Language.

There is more singing, announcements and special music. Then, the moment has arrived. A man steps onto the platform, opens his Bible, and begins to preach God's Holy Word. He, too, is deaf.

God's man, a deaf man - a church planting missionary deaf man – who was trained, ordained and sent out by his church that was established to bring the Deaf to the feet of Jesus.

It is through our senses (touch, taste, sight, sound and smell) that our entire developmental learning takes place. Many times we take for granted the great blessing our senses are for us until one of them is taken away.

Probably the most important sense we have in the development of human interpersonal relationships, language and communication is our sense of hearing.

One of the most famous deaf-blind persons was Helen Keller. She was born in 1880 with normal hearing and vision. However, in February of 1882, at the age of 19 months, she became deaf and blind due to what is now believed to be either scarlet fever or meningitis. After many years of struggles and difficulties, her family contracted a teacher named Anne Sullivan to work specifically with her. Helen had a rough beginning. However, through much patience and love she began learning to read and to write, and she grew to become unquestionably one of the most noted and accomplished deaf and blind persons the world has ever known. I would encourage all who are interested in deafness to read her biographies.

Helen Keller stated:

> *I am just as deaf as I am blind. The problems of deafness are deeper and more complex, if not more important, than those of blindness. Deafness is a much worse misfortune. For it means the loss of the most vital stimulus – the sound of the voice that brings language, sets thoughts astir, and keeps us in the intellectual company of man.*

A blind person to be sure, has a difficult path in life; however, he can openly communicate and assimilate into his nationalistic culture and heritage since there is no language barrier. The blind have no real sub-culture, only very minimal communication barriers and no difficulty with the comprehension of abstract thoughts and ideas.

However, a deaf person lives in a concrete world; a world of separation from his very own family members; a world of silence. The deaf person is a stranger in his own land, yea, even in his own home. Abstract ideas and concepts can be foreign or very difficult to comprehend. His sharp intellect is starved of one of its primary stimuli – hearing. There is a great deal of learning that comes from daily interaction, hearing of conversations, news, songs, intimations, emotions and attitudes, and an infinite amount of teaching that fall upon "deaf" ears.

The greatest event that can occur in a person's life is the day that he or she receives Jesus Christ as Savior and Lord. In terms of eternity, there is no other more lasting or impacting event.

Deafness greatly affects a person's ability to receive, understand and assimilate the Gospel. They cannot listen to the radio, cassette or audio pod-casting preacher. They will not understand the un-interpreted messages of a pastor or televangelist.

Only about 25% to 30% of a preaching service will be understood by the average lip-reading oral deaf person. Which 75% of the Gospel message would you like to exclude? Deaf people can and must be reached with the complete Gospel of the Lord Jesus Christ.

Jorge and Sofia Pozo with Children

The name of the deaf preacher in the story at the beginning of this introduction is Jorge Pozo. His wife Sofia is deaf and they have two young boys, both of whom are hearing.

By the time Jorge was 16, he had only attended schools that taught orally, and that for only five years. He did not know how to read, write or communicate. In fact, he really only knew about ten words. A friend invited him to come to church at *Efata**. He had never heard of *Efata* before. He was fascinated with what he saw. He came back for several weeks and tried hard to understand the sign language that he was watching.

Note: *Efata* is the Spanish translation of the Greek word translated in English *Ephphatha*. It comes from Mark 7:34 where Jesus healed a deaf man. It means "*Be opened*." It is the name of the church, school, orphanage and training center ministry in Lima, Peru, South America. For more information, visit *www.efata.org*.

When Jorge was 17, his parents enrolled him in the Christian school at *Efata* where he truly began to learn words. He also began to be taught the Bible. He was fascinated with the Word of God and read it often. He continued learning new vocabulary words as he went along. Jorge went forward during an invitation because he saw that everyone else was doing it. He claimed to receive Christ as his Saviour. He was baptized; however, according to his own testimony, did not truly understand salvation.

Jorge finished school but left church for a period of two years. He was not happy with his life and remembered the happiness that he had enjoyed when he was at *Efata*. Jorge started coming back to church and during a Bible conference, he trusted the Lord Jesus Christ as his Saviour. He finally understood what salvation meant.

Jorge was an excellent and dedicated student who went on to Bible college at *Efata* where he met his wife Sofia. He graduated, was married, and for a time assisted in the *Efata Baptist Church*, which was founded by Missionary Vernon Miller, himself a pioneering deaf missionary.*

In September of 2000, Pastor Jorge was ordained into the Gospel Ministry. He served as an assistant-pastor at *Efata* for three years. In March of 2003, *Efata Baptist Church* commissioned him as a missionary and sent him and his family out as missionaries to the Deaf.

Jorge and his family are currently serving as missionaries to the Deaf in Huancayo, Peru. *Jorge Pozo is a success story of God's*

Vernon and Velma Miller

Note: For a brief biographical sketch of Missionary Vernon Miller, please read the booklet from the series "*People Who Have Made a Difference in the Deaf World*" - **Number Seven**, published by *Silent Word Ministries* referenced in the back of this book. They have several informative sketches of deaf and hearing pioneers and workers in Deaf ministry and service.

providence and care in the life of a deaf young man who needed to know Jesus.

Both Missionaries, Vernon Miller and Jorge Pozo, are testimonies of the value of investing and surrendering to work among the silent population of the world known as the Deaf. Through this investment, made possible by caring and sacrificial churches and individuals, many Deaf will one day, as Isaiah says, *"hear the words of the book"!* (Isaiah 29:18)

The Deaf can! Set forth in the pages of this book are some basic and practical teachings concerning deafness and Deaf ministry. There are challenges for those who would consider serving the Lord in the wonderful and needed ministry. We MUST make a difference if the Deaf are to have the same opportunity to understand the Gospel message that the hearing have. It is our generation. **It is our time now** to make a difference and reach the Deaf for Christ!

We need a new generation of leadership in Deaf ministry like Vernon Miller and Jorge Pozo; as well as hearing leaders and preachers for the Deaf. We are here *"for such a time as this."* **NOW** is the time to make a difference and *to go INTO THE SILENCE!*

1

DEAFNESS - A BIBLICAL PERSPECTIVE

And the LORD said unto him, Who hath made man's mouth? or who maketh the dumb, or deaf, or the seeing, or the blind? have not I the LORD?

- Exodus 4:11

And again, departing from the coasts of Tyre and Sidon, he came unto the sea of Galilee, through the midst of the coasts of Decapolis. And they bring unto him one that was deaf, and had an impediment in his speech; and they beseech him to put his hand upon him. And he took him aside from the multitude, and put his fingers into his ears, and he spit, and touched his tongue; And looking up to heaven, he sighed, and saith unto him, Ephphatha, that is, Be opened. And straightway his ears were opened, and the string of his tongue was loosed, and he spake plain. And he charged them that they should tell no man: but the more he charged them, so much the more a great deal they published it; And were beyond measure astonished, saying, He hath done all things well: he maketh both the deaf to hear, and the dumb to speak.

- Mark 7:31-37

The Bible has much to say about the Deaf. This first chapter will share with you a Biblical perspective of the importance of the Deaf to God.

The Deaf Are God's Creation

God created the Deaf for His purpose. One might say, "Deafness is due to sin and the sin nature. Thus, it is a direct result of sin's corruption." Hence there would not have been deaf or blind folks had their not been sin. This is true. However, God has used and is using the circumstances of man's fall, and its consequences, to demonstrate his great love for all mankind. He has created special needs people to bring Glory to His name and demonstrate through weakness, that He is strong!

One might inquire, "How could a loving God make a person deaf or blind?" In response, one might ask, "Who made us God's counselors? No person can judge an all mighty all wise God who IS love.

> *Who hath directed the Spirit of the LORD, or being his counsellor hath taught him? With whom took he counsel, and who instructed him, and taught him in the path of judgment, and taught him knowledge, and shewed to him the way of understanding?* -Isaiah 40:13-14

If you look at things through the perspective of a deaf person or a blind person, though there are some limitations placed upon them due to their lack of hearing or seeing, they have the advantage of not having to listen or see the garbage and filth that this world has to offer. In this respect, who has the "handicap"? (*The Deaf do not consider themselves "handicapped." Their deafness is a way of life to them. It is their culture. It is a social issue not a physical one.*)

It is by our perceptions of our physical circumstances or situations that we tend to base our determination of who is blessed or not blessed. There are people wonderfully blessed of God that would tell you so who would not fit into our "normal" mold.

This begs the old saying, "It is better to have loved and lost that love than never to have loved at all." Thus, "It is better to have lived and been saved being deaf, blind, disabled, than never to have lived at all."

Do not pity the Deaf. They are God's handiwork; masterpieces of His own Divine design and purpose to be fulfilled in this life for His ultimate glory, which awaits revelation.

For now we see through a glass, darkly; but then face to face: now I know in part; but then shall I know even as also I am known. - 1Corinthians 13:12

The Deaf have God's Care

Thou shalt not curse the deaf, *nor put a stumblingblock before the blind, but shalt fear thy God: I am the LORD.* - Leviticus 19:14

*The blind receive their sight, and the lame walk, the lepers are cleansed, and **the deaf hear**, the dead are raised up, and the poor have the Gospel preached to them.* - Matthew 11:5

God placed a special command of protection for deaf and blind people. We would be wise to heed it. Jesus showed His love and care for them in His ministry. Should we not show the same?

When you look at what God calls *"pure religion"* in the book of James, you notice a distinct emphasis on caring and helping those who are afflicted. Deaf and blind people, for the most part, would fit into this group of people.

Pure religion and undefiled before God and the Father is this, To visit the fatherless and widows in their affliction, and to keep himself unspotted from the world. - James 1:27

When you work with the Deaf by teaching them language and the Bible way to Heaven, when you take them in, feed them, clothe them and provide a place for them to live and when you care for them, you are practicing *"pure religion."*

It is this author's deep conviction that one of the reasons that God creates and allows what we would call "disadvantaged" people in the world, is to show His true love and character **through us** as we minister and labor for Him. God has given us His ministry of *reconciliation*, so that we would bring glory to His name (2 Corinthians 5:18). Our labor of love should be a testimony to the world of God's care.

Many lost people have been blessed and many saved because of the work among the Deaf at *Efata*. It has provided inroads that otherwise would not have been available. Time after time, people have commented, "You are truly doing the Lord's work here."

Ministry among the Deaf IS the Lord's work. It **IS** part of the great commission. It is ***PURE RELIGION*!**

A few years ago we received a little bundle of love into our home for the Deaf. She was an abandoned little deaf girl of less than two years old. She could not walk and would not look anyone in the eyes. She had developed no personal connection with anyone. She was a sweetheart whose life was stagnated by an uncaring mother and father.

Over time she has made great progress. She leads a normal deaf child's life in a loving adoptive home enjoying her new family, home and care in the United States. She is a very intelligent little girl who has overcome many obstacles. All she needed in her life was  for someone to practice the *pure religion* of the Bible.

God cares about the Deaf and commands us to fear Him in the way we care for them. To ignore this vital ministry in our sphere of influence, in essence, is to fail to demonstrate the fear of God!

Therefore to him that knoweth to do good, and doeth it not, to him it is sin.   - Jam 4:17

There is a great movement in fundamental circles to support only church planting missionaries to the exclusion of all other types. This author humbly disagrees with this mindset. Just as many ministries in the States are multifaceted with paid staff for various ministries, he believes that it is important to support missionaries who are support staff for the church planter; missionaries who would give their lives to practice **pure religion** as the Bible defines it.

Remember, as you invest in children, especially abandoned and neglected children, you are building into them a lifelong love for the things of the Lord and you will be helping to create church planters who might have otherwise been antagonistic to the things of God for the lack of proper Biblical care. Your results may not be immediate, but they will be lasting.

The Deaf Will be God's Consummation

And in that day shall the deaf hear the words of the book, and the eyes of the blind shall see out of obscurity, and out of darkness. - Isaiah 29:18

Then the eyes of the blind shall be opened, and the ears of the deaf shall be unstopped. - Isaiah 35:5

There will be a day when the Deaf shall HEAR with their ears the words of the book and the eyes of the blind will SEE. One would think that this will be a glorious time for all.

However, what exactly will their new or recovered senses hear and see? Which of the following declarations of God would you desire the Deaf to hear for the first time?

This one:

Then shall the King say unto them on his right hand, Come, ye blessed of my Father, inherit the kingdom prepared for you from the foundation of the world, - Matthew 25:34

Or, this one:

Then shall he say also unto them on the left hand, Depart from me, ye cursed, into everlasting fire, prepared for the devil and his angels: -Matthew 25:41

A **lost deaf** man is as equally responsible for his sin as a lost hearing man is! Somebody needs to go tell the Deaf this truth! They **ARE** WITHOUT EXCUSE. They see the same *nature* that we do - a nature that declares the glory of God!

A deaf person will not be able to stand before God at the *Great White Throne* judgment and plead ignorance because of his deafness. "Lord I would have understood if they had just told me!"

The heavens declare the glory of God; and the firmament sheweth his handywork. - Psalm 19:1

The heavens declare his righteousness, and all the people see his glory. - Psalm 97:6

For the invisible things of him from the creation of the world are clearly seen, being understood by the things that are made, even his eternal power and Godhead; so that they are without excuse: - Romans 1:20

In this respect, ministry to the Deaf is no different from ministry to the hearing. It is our responsibility to tell and their responsibility to respond.

There is nothing that negates the responsibility of a deaf person from doing right. It is not a question of not being able to discern right from wrong. They are not mentally challenged in the sense that they cannot understand due to some physiological or organic medical problem. It is a question of access not ability. The same access, which we have to the Gospel, should be afforded to the Deaf. We see God's handiwork and power in nature and in the heavens. For this reason God declares us *"without excuse."* They see the same things we do, and thus are equally without excuse.

In regards to the Gospel and Bible truths, hearing people have one major advantage that helps them to understand better. That advantage is the ability to hear Bible preaching, teaching and exposition.

This is where we must labor to provide accommodations that will help a deaf person overcome the obstacles of his deafness through sign language and education. These accommodations are what we call **Deaf Ministry** – bringing the Deaf to the feet of Jesus by providing opportunity through ministry for them to understand and accept the Gospel of the Lord Jesus Christ!

It is so exciting to listen to the testimonies of deaf adults and children who have accepted Christ as Saviour and to see their eyes of understanding opened. There is nothing like it in the world, especially after you have labored for so long to help them to understand.

If you have ever seen the movie or read the story of Helen Keller, you will remember the climactic moment when she understood for the first time what the movements and hand shapes being presented to her in her little hand meant:

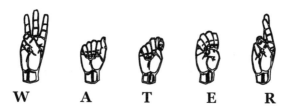

W   A   T   E   R

You might even have been touched as the music began to crescendo and Helen's "hands" of understanding were opened as Anne Sullivan began fingerspelling words into Helen's hand and Helen understood!

– PUMP

– HELEN

– TEACHER

– MOTHER

What excitement! What joy and tears! All of it experienced because a little girl who was deaf and blind could now understand.

The Word of God states:

> *What man of you, having an hundred sheep, if he lose one of them, doth not leave the ninety and nine in the wilderness, and go after that which is lost, until he find it? 5 And when he hath found it, he layeth it on his shoulders, rejoicing. 6 And when he cometh home, he calleth together his friends and neighbours, saying unto them, Rejoice with me; for I have found my sheep which was lost. 7 **I say unto you, that likewise joy shall be in heaven over one sinner that repenteth,** more than over ninety and nine just persons, which need no repentance.* - Luke 15:4-7

If there will be such joy in heaven over one sinner who repents, how much more over one deaf sinner who repents, for whom such great barriers had to be broken down to allow him to understand the precious Gospel, MUCH JOY!

A highly recommend movie concerning deafness and salvation is *When Silence Speaks*, produced by the *Bill Rice Ranch* in *Murfreesboro, Tennessee. It is the* story of Gordy Folkrod; a true story of a deaf man who was struggling with life and trying to understand the Cross. It chronicles the events that led to his salvation and how he became a witness for Christ. Though he could not read or write, he was saved through the care of a pastor and friends. After his salvation, he built a cross and set it up across a road. When a car would pass by, he would stop it. He would then point to the cross he set up and then to the occupant's hearts. He would then show them a highlighted passage of the Word of God. *(You* can purchase this video through *Silent Word Ministries.* There address is on the *Recommended Resources* page of this book.)

God cares about the Deaf and the Deaf can care about God and the things of God. It is our responsibility to be a witness and help to make it possible for "silence" to speak!

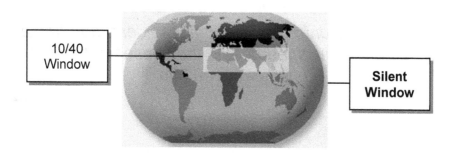

2

THE
SILENT
WINDOW

And they bring unto him one that was deaf, and had an impediment in his speech; and they beseech him to put his hand upon him.

- Mark 7:32

A young boy named Gustavo lived on the streets of Lima, Peru trying to sell candy on the buses just to survive. He would jump on the buses while they were waiting to depart and sell his candies. He became a regular feature on some of the routes. One day he did not show up and the bus drivers were curious as to what had happened to him. Gustavo was found in a ditch beaten and robbed of what little he had.

Gustavo is deaf and was abandoned by his family. He had been away from home for over three years. He was turned over to the police who eventually brought him to Efata. Research was done and Gustavo's father was found. He told us that his mother did not want him and that he wanted him to stay at Efata.

Gustavo knew no language and other than basic gestures could not communicate. Now, Gustavo is an extremely bright young man. He trusted Christ as his personal Saviour and followed the Lord in baptism.

Gustavo has overcome some very serious obstacles in his life. With the help and support of a Bible-believing ministry to the Deaf, Gustavo's life has been changed eternally.

There has been much said and studied about the *10/40 Window* as it relates to missions. This is a valid mission emphasis and should not be ignored. Thankfully, many missionaries, churches and mission agencies are beginning to focus and develop strategies to reach this under-evangelized region between 10 and 40 degrees above the equator of people groups and nations. It is claimed that over 1.3 billion people live in this region that have little or no hope of hearing the Gospel.

There is also another "window" of missions that is just as needy and just as difficult to reach. It is a window that extends to the farthest southern degree of the globe to its most northern cousin. This window is not only centered in Asia but circles the Globe. It is **The Silent Window**.

This window consists of approximately 400 million deaf and hard-of-hearing persons who are in the world today, of which approximately 68 million are profoundly deaf people with little or no hearing ability at all. Depending on the country, the Deaf and hard of hearing population could be as little as 6% to as much as 10% of a country's population. This figure amounts to the third largest people group in the world.

Here are some interesting facts:

- Only two percent of the Deaf in the world profess to be Christians. *- Deaf Ministry Worldwide*

- The greatest health issue in the United States is **loss of hearing** – affecting more Americans than heart disease, cancer, venereal disease, blindness, tuberculosis, multiple sclerosis and kidney disease put together! *- National Institute for Health – Sylvia Porter*

- There is approximately one deaf and 20 hard-of-hearing for every 1000 persons in Africa. *- Christian Mission for the Deaf*

- If all of the Deaf of the world lived in one place, it would be the third largest country in the world.

The Deaf live in a silent world where they blend into the background and mostly are forgotten or ignored.

In the United States of America, the opportunities for education and advancement abound for the Deaf. The legal stature and status of deaf people is highly advanced and Deaf culture is very well established. There is very little limit to what a deaf person can achieve. There are universities, colleges, state schools and institutions - public and private, as well as a plethora of advocacy groups dedicated to the education and vocational training of the Deaf as well as the preservation of their cultural heritage.

North America has many ministries, evangelists, churches, mission organizations and fellowships that reach out to the Deaf. For years, the American Christian community has made great strides in their evangelization throughout the United States.

Unfortunately, this same attention and care for global New Testament missions and ministry among the Deaf has not been demonstrated. There are many good faithful missionaries on the foreign field who are working with deaf and hard-of-hearing people groups. However, these numbers are quite small when compared to the total number of independent Baptist missionaries.

According to Dr. Charles Keen, Founder of *First Bible International* (www.firstbible.net), there are an estimated 3000 Independent Baptist missionaries or missionary families today sent out from the United States. *

It is this author's estimation that less than 50 of those missionaries or missionary families are reaching the Deaf on foreign fields. That means only 1.7% of the Independent Baptist missionary effort is reaching the Deaf.

Note: Dr. Keen advises that this number is very subjective, as it does not include missionaries sent out by their local churches who would not be counted in mission board statistics. In addition, some boards count each individual as a missionary (husband and wife count as two missionaries) and others count one family as one missionary unit (husband and wife count as one missionary unit).

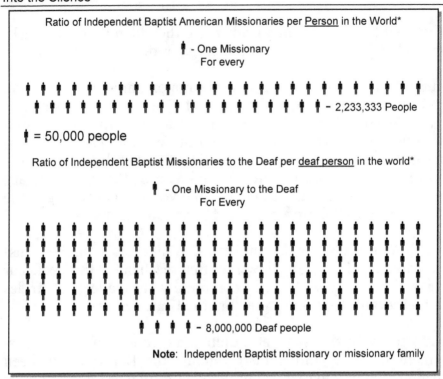

Ratio of Independent Baptist American Missionaries per Person in the World*

- One Missionary For every — 2,233,333 People

= 50,000 people

Ratio of Independent Baptist Missionaries to the Deaf per deaf person in the world*

- One Missionary to the Deaf For Every — 8,000,000 Deaf people

Note: Independent Baptist missionary or missionary family

That means that there is approximately one Independent Baptist Missionary for every 2,233,333 people on the earth. However, when you consider specifically Deaf missions, there is only one foreign Independent Baptist missionary to the Deaf for every 8,000,000 **deaf** people.

To give you another perspective of the need for missionaries to the Deaf; all of the approximately 202 countries on the earth have Deaf in them. <u>ALL</u> of them have a distinct language and sub-culture apart from the hearing people around them.

While there are approximately 15 North American Independent Baptist missionaries for every country in the world, there is only **one** North American independent Baptist missionary to the Deaf for every **four countries**.

Statistics can be misleading and the numbers are <u>very subjective</u>. Again, they are presented here to add context to the need. However, when you view the vast difference in the numbers, you can only conclude – there is a great unreached mission field waiting for laborers; a silent mission field of deaf people.

Definition of Deafness

Webster's 1913 Dictionary defines deafness as:

Incapacity of perceiving sounds; the state of the organs which prevents the impression which constitute hearing; want of sense of hearing. *

The Britannica Concise Encyclopedia defines deafness as:

Partial or total inability to hear. In conduction deafness, the passage of sound vibrations through the ear is interrupted. The obstacle may be earwax, a ruptured eardrum, or stapes fixation, which prevents the stapes bone from transmitting sound vibrations to the inner ear. In sensorineural deafness, a defect in the sensory cells of the inner ear (e.g., injury by excessive noise) or in the vestibulocochlear or eighth cranial nerves prevents the transmission of sound impulses to the auditory centre in the brain. Some deaf people are helped by hearing aids or cochlear implants; others can learn to communicate with sign language and/or lip reading. *

Note: Citations were taken from Answers.com. Further detailed definitions for deafness can be found on their website at: www.answers.com/topic/deafness

To understand deafness further, here are some terms and their definitions as presented on the website *Church Planting Village.net*. You can read their entire article regarding developing a Deaf ministry on their website referenced in the back of this book in the Recommended Resources section.

Hearing impaired – A blanket word, used by hearing persons to explain the hearing loss of a person. This term is considered to be "politically correct" by hearing people; however, it is offensive to those belonging to the Deaf community. They prefer to be identified as "Deaf" or "Hard of Hearing." It is best not to use this term.

Hard of Hearing – This term is used to explain that a person can hear sounds if they are made louder. They have hearing, which is usable. For this reason, these people are rightly called "hard of hearing."

Congenital deafness – This phrase describes deafness, which begins at birth. The deafness may have occurred before or during childbirth. Congenital deafness is caused either by illness in the mother (e.g. rubella during pregnancy), heredity or injury sustained at birth.

Adventitious deafness – This is deafness which occurs in the individual born with normal hearing but who later loses his hearing through sickness or injury. When a person with normal hearing loses his hearing this is called "adventitious deafness." It is also called "acquired deafness" or, as the deaf would sign, "Became deaf."

Accidents – Childhood accidents, such as a blow to the head, can possibly cause deafness. Explosions and other loud noises are also possible causes of deafness.

Prelingual deafness – This term refers to deafness which comes before normal verbal language development occurs. If a person becomes deaf before verbal language develops, this gives the deaf child a difficult beginning in acquiring language through his ears. Many times a deaf child develops minimal or almost no language before he enters school. Trying to make up for the years lost is difficult. Spoken language is difficult for the prelingually deaf person. It is acquired with much difficulty, if acquired at all. If it is possible for the prelingually deaf person to communicate clearly verbally, then it is good to encourage him to communicate verbally as much as possible.

Postlingual deafness – This term refers to deafness occurring after normal verbal language has developed. This child has developed a reservoir of spoken language, English syntax and grammar. Communication is much easier and clearer for him and with him than with the prelingually deaf child. With the postlingually deaf child or adult, it is important to work to retain as much of his speech as possible.

Profound deafness – Profound deafness means a hearing loss in the normal speech range so severe that even with a hearing aid a profoundly deaf person cannot hear speech.

Community – Is a general social system in which a group of people lives together, share common goals, and carry out certain responsibilities to each other.

Deaf Community – A Deaf community is a group of people who lives in a particular location, shares the common goals of its membership, and in various ways, works toward achieving these goals. A Deaf community may include persons who are not themselves deaf, but who actively support the goals of the community, and work with deaf people to achieve them.

Deafness as a Cultural Group

What is culture? Culture is our beliefs, traits, behaviors, societal norms and language, which are transmitted socially.

There is American culture, Japanese culture, Pre-Inca culture, Black culture and so on. Each culture is rich with their own distinct elements such as language, folklore, cuisine, storytelling, dress and beliefs.

One great misunderstanding is that since deaf people are citizens of a certain country, that their culture, language and education will be the same as the hearing people around them. While this may be true to some degree as it relates to their manner of dress, the food they eat and the way they build their homes, it is not a complete reality.

The Deaf hold in common many of the cultural elements of their native country or people group; but not all. That is why this author states that they are their own sub-culture and have distinct cultural elements, which are transmitted within their sub-culture that the larger broader culture does not share. These unique elements revolve around their deafness, language and social structures.

There are many Native American groups living in the United States. Although these Native American groups share some American cultural norms, they also enjoy their own very unique sub-cultural norms. The same is true for the Deaf.

Deafness as its own culture adds many unique challenges to Deaf missions. Anyone desiring to reach the Deaf for Christ must learn about this rich sub-culture and develop an understanding of its differences.

As stated in the *Preface*, **d**eaf and **D**eaf have two very distinct connotations. Those who refer to themselves as **d**eaf are generally speaking of living with the physical disability of deafness. Those who speak of themselves as **D**eaf are speaking of themselves as being **culturally** Deaf – a people group. One can be hearing and be culturally Deaf. By the same token, one can be deaf and not be a part of Deaf culture.

Deaf culture is a sub-culture in every country. In fact, the Deaf of one country have much in common culturally with the Deaf of other countries; sometimes more so than with their own hearing nationals. This is a profound uniqueness in what is Deaf culture.

One could liken it to a Bible-believing Christian in the United States having more in common with a Bible-believing Christian in South America regardless of the language, national heritage, customs and norms of the two countries. Being brothers and sisters in Christ transcends nationalistic prejudices and pride.

That same Bible-believing Christian would have greater conflict with the unconverted North American culture of his lost "American" neighbors, than with his brother-in-Christ a world away.

It is the same with Deaf culture. It has, in many ways, more in common with Deaf cultures around the world than with the hearing cultures of the countries where they are born.

Many times in the ministry of *Efata* in Peru visitors who are Deaf come by from various countries. People have come from North America, Britain, Spain, Sweden, Switzerland, Germany, and other South and Central American countries, etc.; all of whom enjoyed greatly the companionship of other Deaf.

Though the languages of their home countries were different from Peruvian Sign Language, they interacted and were in their comfort zones among Peruvian Deaf. It was as if they were visiting long lost relatives who spoke in a different language. They would learn each other's fingerspelling and basic signs and enjoy the challenge and richness of it all.

A good example of this is the struggle that took place in October of 2006 where *Gallaudet University* had a major protest over the choice to replace Dr. I. King Jordan as President of the University.

Dr. Jane Fernandes, who was born deaf, was selected as the new president to take over from the retiring Dr. Jordan. The problem was not that she was not deaf. The problem was that she was not considered deaf enough. She was not **D**eaf. She learned sign language at the age of 23 and was not considered to be culturally Deaf enough by many in the American Deaf culture.

Deaf people do not consider their deafness as a disability. They consider it a culture to be cherished, respected and loved. Their sign language is an inseparable part of that culture just as our spoken language is of ours.

The following portion of an article titled *Unspoken Bond* from *The Columbus Dispatch* dated Monday January 2nd 2006 by Encarnacion Pyle, gives us a wonderful example of the mindset of Deaf culture:

He clenches his tiny fists, takes a gulp of air and lets out a shriek his parents think can be heard throughout the hospital.

Like most other newborns, Yale has a healthy set of lungs, but his audiologist wonders whether he can hear himself screaming.

Lindsay Slivka tapes an electrode behind each of his ears and on his forehead, which is scrunched like a little old man's. Then she places a small probe into Yale's right ear canal and a pacifier in his mouth.

He contentedly sucks as the probe emits several tones that should cause the hair cells in his inner ears to bend, creating an echo that Slivka's equipment can pick up.

"He's not moving," says his father, Jeff Frink. "He must be stone deaf."

"Don't worry," Slivka says, soothingly. "Most babies sleep through it."

Slivka performs another test and checks the results twice before giving Frink and his wife, Lisa, the news: Yale has failed.

Smiles spread across their faces.

"He is perfect, perfect!" Mr. Frink shouts, wildly waving his arms while dancing around the labor recovery room in Riverside Methodist Hospital. "Some people would say he failed, but to us, he passed. He scored an F for fantastic!"

The Frinks, both deaf, have 10 other children with hearing impairments. For them, deafness is a part of their cultural identity — and a point of pride.

"It's what we know," Mrs. Frink, 44, signs to an interpreter who is helping the couple communicate with Slivka. "It's normal."

"It's not a disability or medical condition that needs to be fixed," adds Mr. Frink, 47. "It's something that makes one of a thousand Americans special. It's called 'Deaf Culture.'"

Opening the Silent Window

It is this author's desire that we as Bible Believing Christians, open this Silent Window that we may reach through it to those on the other side who cannot hear the Gospel of the Lord Jesus Christ.

There is only ONE "Great Commission." In the book of Matthew, the Bible says, *"Go ye therefore, and teach all nations..."* Nations can be understood to mean "People groups." Deaf are a unique people group, culturally, linguistically, and demographically. However, they have the same ONE need that all humanity has – salvation!

In Mark 16:15 the Bible says, *"And he said unto them, Go ye into all the world, and preach the Gospel to every creature."* This mandate reminds us of our responsibility to reach deaf people with the Gospel no matter where they live. It does not release us from that responsibility because there are unique linguistic or cultural hurdles to overcome. We cannot and must not recuse ourselves because the task is great or difficult!

The Lord Jesus Christ went to a different people and culture group, to minister to **one** deaf man (Mark 7:32). We should be willing to be trained, equipped and motivated to reach deaf people as well; no matter where the Lord sends us.

No matter how you look at it, the Deaf are greatly under reached. It is a global *"white already to harvest"* mission field that is waiting dedicated, heroic and pioneering missionaries; the likes of Hudson Taylor, William Carey, David Livingstone, Bob Himes, Vernon Miller and Ray Bradley to carry the Light so Deaf can HEAR!

If you are a young person being called of God to do a pioneering, challenging and fulfilling mission work, pray that God will touch your heart to reach the Deaf around the world. If YOU will not, WHO WILL?

The Deaf especially need dedicated young men who will volunteer to go and invest their lives in Deaf missions. Remember Isaiah was not called to be a prophet to Israel and the nations, he VOLUNTEERED!

Also I heard the voice of the Lord, saying, Whom shall I send, and who will go for us? Then said I, Here am I; send me.
                                                    - Isaiah 6:8

On a final note, this author would like to share another thought from Helen Keller and then adjust her thought to a Christian perspective.

Helen Keller stated:

The public must learn that the blind man is neither genius nor a freak nor an idiot. He has a mind that can be educated, a hand which can be trained, ambitions which it is right for him to strive to realize, and it is the duty of the public to help him make the best of himself so that he can win light through work.

Adaptation with a Christian perspective:

The Christian World must learn that the deaf man is lost and condemned to Hell. He has a mind that can be educated in the Gospel, hands that can be trained to share that Gospel and an eternity to live that he has a right to realize through Christ. It is the DUTY of Christians to see he has the opportunity to HEAR the LIGHT of the Gospel through missions.

Deaf ministry is one of the hardest of all ministries; Deaf ministry on the foreign field is even harder. The missionary must learn two languages and cultures and two ways of thinking and working that are distinct. He must confront difficult challenges and frustrations very unique to Deaf missions. The challenge is daunting. However, as the scriptures say: *"greater is he that is in you, than he that is in the world."* (1 John 4:4) and *"I can do all things through Christ which strengtheneth me."* (Philippians 4:13) God equips us for the task. We just need to go and do it!

We must motivate and work together to open this vast *Silent Window* so the LIGHT of the glorious Gospel can shine in the hearts of the Deaf as well.

Helen Keller with Dr. Alexander Graham Bell
Photo from Penn Library/Digital Library Projects
http://*digital*.library.upenn.edu/women/keller/life/76.gif

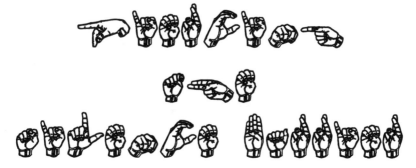

PIERCING
THE
SILENCE
BARRIER

(HOW TO REACH THE DEAF)

How then shall they call on him in whom they have not believed? and how shall they believe in him of whom they have not heard? and how shall they hear without a preacher?

- Romans 10:14

In April of 1968 a deaf missionary by the name of Vernon Miller went to Peru, South America to begin a ministry to the Deaf. He tried multiple times to start a church but the lack of Peruvian Sign Language and different cultural obstacles prevented him from having any success.

Thankfully, these obstacles did not prevent Vernon from finding solutions. After what seemed to be several fruitless years, he and another American missionary were praying in the other missionaries home concerning this when a knock came at the door. There standing at the entrance was a woman who knew of two deaf boys who needed to be in school but did not know where to turn for help. Through the providence of God, she was directed to the right door at the right time as an answer to prayer.

Those two boys and others that followed became the first "crack" that would break the "Silence Barrier" in Peru. Since that time, decades ago, hundreds of deaf children have been educated and hearing interpreters and workers trained. Today the Deaf of Peru are making great strides and advances in advocacy for their culture and more importantly, many Deaf are being saved and ministered to throughout the country; all because of the efforts of one deaf missionary with a vision and those who followed after.

Naturally, one of the first difficulties of deaf outreach is finding the Deaf. Many pastors and people have stated that in their area of ministry, they rarely, if ever, meet a deaf person. Thus, the need to develop Deaf outreach is not recognized. The old saying, "*Out of sight, out of mind*," really does ring true in Deaf ministry.

This develops a sense that it is not worth putting a great deal of effort, education and time into learning sign language and Deaf culture as there is no real need for so few Deaf. The reality is that there are probably more deaf people than you realize in your city. You just have not met them yet.

On several occasions, this author has participated in symposiums offered by the Congress of Peru or conferences by various governmental and non-governmental organizations regarding the work that was being done to advance laws in support of the disabled populations of Peru. In these meetings presentations were made regarding a wide range of issues for the disabled from accessibility to education. Present were people who were blind, mobility challenged, developmentally disabled and with a variety of other disabilities.

Each group of disabled people where easily recognized except for one, the Deaf. There were several deaf people in attendance who could not be distinguished from any other hearing person present. Were it not for the interpreters, one may not have thought to consider that their might be deaf people participating.

Deafness is a silent and undistinguishable disability or culture (depending on your perspective). For this reason the Deaf many times go unnoticed and unreached.

Here are a few **misconceptions** that need to be addressed if any church or individual is going to have an effective ministry to the Deaf.

1. The Deaf are mentally retarded or incapable of understanding the Gospel.

As this author has stated so many times, the Deaf do not lack *capacity*; they lack *opportunity*! There is a great difference.

Capacity is your ability to learn and grow with the mental and physical abilities that you have. Opportunity is the chance to exercise your capacity, which leads to learning and growth.

Deaf people cannot hear, but that does not mean they cannot learn or achieve. They live in a concrete world where abstract concepts at times are difficult for them to understand. However, with proper education and opportunity, this can be overcome.

Have you ever heard this chorus: *"There's honey in the Rock dear brother, there's honey in the Rock for you."*

This phrase of that beautiful song is very abstract. If you were to look at it in a concrete way, there would be no understanding it. For the Deaf it is not natural to understand the abstracts of this phrase to mean that there are wonderful, sweet blessings (honey) in the Lord Jesus Christ (the Rock) unless they are taught.

How about this one: *"He hideth my soul in the cleft of the rock, Where rivers of pleasure I see."*

How would you interpret this phrase? It takes some creative deconstruction to bring it from its abstract poetic form to a literal translatable form for the Deaf. Take some time and have some fun; write down your understanding of this phrase.

If you lived in a concrete world where abstract thinking was almost non-existent what would you think of that song?

With this understanding, you should know that the Deaf can and have been taught to understand what the phrases of these songs mean. They are a challenge to interpret for even a seasoned interpreter, but they can be made understandable.

There are deaf engineers, doctors, technicians, lawyers, preachers; professionals in every career field and vocation with extremely advanced degrees in the Arts and Sciences who are deaf.

Please understand that there are some deaf people who suffer from multiple physiological issues. Their deafness is just one factor of their physiological makeup. One should not gauge the entire deaf population by the experiences he or she may have had with someone who has multiple issues in their lives. Those who are deaf and have other physiological needs require special care.

Someone might say that the Deaf cannot understand the Gospel and thus have an automatic *"Get out of Hell free"* card. This is not the case. Deaf can and do understand the Gospel when presented to them in a language they can understand.

If you are an English speaker and did not know the Saviour and someone told you about Jesus in a foreign language that you did not know, you would not understand it. Does that mean you would be exempted from the penalty of sin if you were without Christ? No, it does not. It just identifies you as one of the billions of Hell-deserving sinners who have a need for a missionary to bring you the Gospel *in a language that **you** understand*.

2. The Deaf can just sit on the front row and read the lips of the preacher.

Contrary to popular belief, the majority of deaf people **CANNOT** read lips effectively. This includes even those who have gone to a school that teaches the Oral Method.

A preacher generally moves and turns his face as he is speaking and thus the deaf person misses much of what is said. Some preachers are very difficult to understand or lip-read because of their facial structure and vocal or physical clarity in the formation of their words. This makes it difficult for the deaf person to be fed spiritually. In addition, the distance away from the preacher to the congregant may, in and of itself, hinder one's ability to read his lips effectively.

Once while this author was with some deaf and hearing friends, one of his deaf friends was lip-reading a conversation by a hearing person who knew no signs. The hearing person was telling a joke and the deaf person could not make any sense of it because he could not track or follow well the lips of the person speaking and the abstract concepts of the joke were impossible to assimilate for him. Finally, this deaf friend asked for the joke to be interpreted so he could understand it and know why everyone else was laughing.

3. If we provide an interpreter, they will come.

Several years ago a movie came out about baseball where the main character was told: "If you build it, they will come." This may work in the movies, however, it is not always so in real life. Churches provide a preacher; but this does not draw everyone to come out to the church to hear him.

Reaching the Deaf is about building relationships and trust. Deaf people by nature are generally careful in their relationships with hearing people. The Deaf have been taken advantage of or "babied" so much by the hearing.

Many interpreters begin with good intentions, but later they quit or move on for various reasons. The Deaf generally tend to take a "wait and see" attitude regarding interpreters and interpreter ministries. The Deaf want to see if a stable ministry that will last is being provided or if it will be a "flash in the pan."

Deaf people greatly enjoy fellowship and companionship. They are a very social people group. Just providing an interpreter is not going to reach the Deaf for Christ, though it is not a bad start.

4. We can give the Deaf Gospel tracts, which they can read, and therefore trust Christ.

The average reading level for a deaf person age 17-18 in the United States is the 4.0 grade level of hearing students*. On the average, writing and reading are not the strong suits of the Deaf. Unfortunately, in most third world countries, the majority of the Deaf have never been taught how to read or write, and those that do, for the most part are on a very elementary level where they misunderstand the very words that they are reading or do not put

---

Note: Gallaudet Research Institute. 1996. Stanford Achievement Test, 9th Edition, Form S, Norms Booklet for Deaf and Hard-of-Hearing Students. (Including Conversions of Raw Score to Scaled Score & Grade Equivalent and Age-based Percentile Ranks for Deaf and Hard-of-Hearing Students.) Washington, DC: Gallaudet University.

---

the words together properly to understand the concept the words are attempting to convey. Thus, taking a tract or Bible and giving it to them to read is not going to be very effective. Even illustrated tracts, *Evangecubes*, Wordless Books and flashcard drawings can be "busy" and a bit difficult to understand without context and "some man to guide them."

5. The Deaf can never be effective leaders in ministry

<u>Nothing could be further from the truth</u>. There are many excellent Deaf leaders in Independent Baptist circles. Some have earned doctorate degrees and many have honorary doctorates for their life's work and sacrifice. These are men and women who are missionaries, pastors, evangelists, college founders and presidents, teachers and leaders in North America and around the world.

As stated before, in the secular professions there are engineers, doctors, lawyers, scientist, researchers, contractors, university presidents, small business owners and the list goes on. In every facet and walk of life deaf people have excelled where they have seized the opportunities they were afforded.

Some Differences Between Deaf and Hearing Worlds

There are many differences between the Deaf world and the hearing world. This list is by no means exhaustive, just illustrative.

Deaf humor – Since much of hearing humor is based on word play, the Deaf do not "get it" most of the time. Many times Deaf humor is just as "interesting" to our hearing minds. So as to not feel out of place, many deaf people will laugh when the see everyone else laughing, but in reality, they did not get the joke.

Deaf language – The language of the Deaf is a visual/gesture-based language. Deaf have their own idiomatic expressions. American Sign Language is a recognized foreign language in many states and schools. It is based on hand shapes, movements, sign placement and location, facial expressions and their intensity as well as gestures.

Hearing language depends mostly on tone, volume and the formation as well as timing of sounds. It also uses expressions and body language.

Deaf are naturally frank and undiplomatic – They tell you what they think. Deaf people are notoriously straightforward in their conversations and expressions. If you ask their opinion (and even if you don't), be prepared to get it! Understand, they DO NOT mean to intentionally hurt or harm with their words. They just lack the cultural and social graces that we hearing people enjoy and expect because of our language and culture.

Deaf are visually stimulated – This is for obvious reasons. Hearing folks are visually AND aurally stimulated.

Deaf music is rhythm or beat-based – Deaf music has three elements - timing, flow and coordination. Hearing music has three elements as well - melody, harmony and rhythm.

Deaf are very cliquish – They tend to be wary of new people entering their culture. Once in, hearing people are generally well accepted as long as they maintain their respect for the culture of the Deaf.

Deaf tend to have difficulty with forgetting wrongs or offenses even after forgiveness – This is a strong difficulty to overcome. Confidence is easy to gain, but once lost, it is very difficult to regain.

Deaf will generally be slower learners - It is the process of learning that is slower, as one of the primary stimuli for learning is absent – hearing. They can learn the same things as hearing but depending on the concept being taught, it may take considerably longer to get it across, especially if it is an abstract concept.

Deaf think differently – The average deaf person generally does not think in words or sentences but in visual concepts. Highly educated Deaf however, can and do think much like hearing people.

Some Don'ts in Deaf Ministry

- Do not treat the Deaf as sub-normal. They are not. They are just like hearing people with the same loves, hates, feelings, strengths, weaknesses as well as spiritual, emotional and physical needs.

- Do not talk down to the Deaf from a superior "hearing" perspective. You do not like it when someone talks to you condescendingly. Well, neither do the Deaf.

- Do not baby the Deaf. The Deaf CAN! They do not need co-dependents or enablers. In our quest to help the Deaf socially, we have at times created a dependency that is not healthy or conducive to forming leaders.

- Do not assume anything with the Deaf. Treat them as you wish to be treated. The *Golden Rule* is a good Biblical principle with which to be guided.

- Do not ignore their presence when talking with others. Be sensitive to their presence when carrying on a conversation with others. They are very sensitive to this because it shows a lack of respect for them if you talk without including them in the conversation if they are present. (This is also a problem with different verbal language groups as well.)

  The reverse is also true. It is just as rude for deaf people to carry on a conversation and not try to include a new hearing signer when present into their conversation. This door swings both ways.

- Do not assume that they understand you just because they shake their heads affirmatively. You can even ask if they understand and they will indicate yes when they do not.

  This is NOT only a Deaf problem. Everyone does this from time to time. We do not wish to be looked down upon because we did not understand. It would be better to say that you did not understand and ask the person to repeat what they said as opposed to getting the information wrong and suffering the consequences of this ignorance.

- Do not forget that this is ministry and ministry means sacrifice and death to self. You must be willing to die to self in any ministry. However, in Deaf ministry, you should be a "walking corpse" where your feelings are concerned.

How Do We Prepare to Reach the Deaf?

Deaf ministry on the whole is a great deal more difficult than hearing ministry. It has a very unique set of challenges and requires an exceptional amount of patience. As stated before, the Deaf are a separate sub-culture in any country, including in the United States.

- Remember when you are working with the Deaf you are investing in a mission field – EVEN IN THE UNITED STATES!

- Have a genuine care and interest for Deaf ministry.

- Determine the type of Deaf ministry that meets the needs and realities that you have in your church or area. These different ministry types will be explained further in Chapter Five. Here is a general overview:
  - o One-on-one ministry
  - o Interpreted ministry
  - o Deaf ministry as a department in your church
    - With a layman servant to the Deaf
    - With an ordained pastor to the Deaf
      - Full time
      - Part time
      - Voluntary
  - o Deaf Church

- Learn all you can about the Deaf and their culture.

- o Seek out and participate in deaf community workshops.

- o Attend Deaf story-telling and cultural events.

- o Locate and get to know Deaf assistance and cultural organizations and associations.

- o Contact other churches with Deaf outreach programs or other ministries to the Deaf and ask them for their insights.

- o Read books and resource materials about Deaf culture and deafness. There is a wealth of information available on the internet regarding deafness and Deaf culture and community issues.

- Facilitate sign language learning.

  - o Request training in Deaf ministry and sign language from a ministry or missionary that provides it.

  - o Take advantage of the resources provided by your local library.

  - o Enroll in a sign language course offered by your local community or state colleges.

  - o Find a deaf friend and learn from them.

  - o Attend workshops, seminars and Deaf awareness and cultural events; which are provided by local, state and national institutions; government agencies as well as other religious, educational and private organizations.

- Pray that God will call and use your dedicated and bright young people for Deaf ministry.

- Be a positive source of encouragement and motivation to those who are working or training to work in this ministry.

How Do We Find the Deaf?

There are many ways to find the Deaf. Here are some ideas that may be helpful. Not all of the ideas work everywhere. This is just a brief overview. In Chapter Seven we will address some of these in more detail.

- The most effective way to find the Deaf is through other Deaf.

- Locate schools for the Deaf in your area.

- Look for *Deaf Child* signs.

- Review the phone book for Deaf service centers, interpreter agencies or outreaches.

- Ask around. Many Deaf can be found simply by asking.

- Canvas areas – this, of course, can also be used as a good soul-winning opportunity.

- Check with government agencies that work with the disabled.

- In the U.S., check the phone company for phone books for the Deaf. Florida, for example has a statewide phone book for the Deaf.

- Walk around large shopping areas and be observant for people using sign language.

- Check with local bowling alleys. Deaf people love to bowl and have their own leagues or times when they meet to bowl.

- Frequent other popular gathering areas. The Deaf community may have a day and time where they meet in these places on a weekly or monthly basis.

Ministering to the Deaf

Remember, the needs of the Deaf spiritually are exactly the same as the needs for the hearing. They are lost and in need of the Saviour. They need someone to care enough to bring them to the feet of Jesus.

In many countries, especially third-world countries, before you can ever reach the Deaf with the Gospel, you may have to invest a great deal of time and resources in their education.

- Teaching them a language

- Teaching them to read and write

- Teaching them life skills
    - Personal care
    - Interpersonal relations
    - Basic right from wrong

- Teaching them the concept of God and salvation

Many Deaf already come from abusive backgrounds. The main thing that you can teach them is the love of the Lord Jesus Christ in your attitude and actions toward them.

Even a new signer or worker among the Deaf, who is a dedicated Christian servant, can teach the best language of all, the **Language of LOVE.**

At *Efata* many boys and girls have come from abusive or destructive backgrounds and family situations, whose lives have been wholly changed by God's love and care shown through the hands and hearts of those who serve in this wonderful ministry among the Deaf in Peru.

To give you an example, there was a little boy that lived at *Efata* named Freddy. Freddy came from a split home where the mother and father were both drug addicts. Neither could stand the other.

Freddy was caught in the middle. When he first arrived, we had to hide the glue that was in his classroom from him. When no one was looking, he would get it out and start sniffing it. At *Efata* he learned the love of Christ and found acceptance and salvation.

Preparing Materials and Presentations

The most important criteria to remember when preparing materials for the Deaf is that they are *visual learners*. All materials should be prepared with this in mind.

Here are several guidelines for preparing lessons and materials for teaching and preaching to the Deaf.

- Keep your lessons on a basic language level. Teach at the median level of your Deaf and privately tutor those who are lagging behind or excelling and have a desire for more.

- Be as visual as possible in the preparation of your materials. Use clear images and aids.

- Make your fonts in your handouts large enough to be read well. Be careful not to use cursive or decorative fonts that are hard to read. Many Deaf also have problems with vision.

- Use Presentation software such as PowerPoint or overheads when possible.

- When you prepare tracts, try to use a great deal of clear graphics and logical progressions. Try to size things for easy visibility.

- Use whiteboards, flip charts, drawings, flannelgraph, etc.; whatever you have available to illustrate and emphasize your lesson and points.

- Do not overload them with information. Try to focus on one main point per lesson with clearly defined and easily explained sub-points.

- When possible and appropriate, provide lesson sheets they can use to fill in as you teach. Keep them involved in the learning process.

- Try to incorporate illustrations that the Deaf themselves can be involved in and materials that they can use so as to keep the learning process interactive and alive.

In most cases your written material should be at an appropriate level so that the Deaf can understand what is written; again, understanding that many Deaf do not have the opportunity for a good education in many parts of the world and even in some parts of the United States. Use words that can easily be signed.

Interpreting

The number one need in reaching any people is communication – the ability to pass concepts from one person to another across a spectrum of differences. It is one of the strongest unifying powers. That is why God confounded language at the Tower of Babel because as the Bible says:

> *And the LORD said, Behold, the people is one, and they have all one language; and this they begin to do: and now nothing will be restrained from them, which they have imagined to do.* - Genesis 11:6

Thus the primary focus for any worker with the Deaf is language development on the part of the worker and in many cases the Deaf. *Learn their language well.*

Remember - Sign language is NOT just an advanced form of gestures. It is a *language* with its own structure, syntax, idiomatic expressions and vocabulary. As stated before, concepts are formed by hand shape, movement and placement, body language, expressions and their intensity coupled with non-verbal indicators such as puffed cheeks, raised eyebrows and pursed lips. We hearing people use a great deal of these non-verbal cues in our conversations as well. However, we depend mainly on the use of verbal tones, inflections and intensity.

To be a good interpreter (preacher or teacher for that matter) for the Deaf, one must be willing to put aside their natural tendencies not to want to look foolish. It is extremely rare to see someone criticize an able, aggressive and animated interpreter.

Image from *Deaf Workers' Handbook* by Maxine Jeffries

Be *alive and passionate* when you *interpret*. Let the passion (or lack thereof) of the person who is speaking ring out of your being through your hands, expressions and body language.

Remember, you are an ACCOMMODATION for the Deaf. You are translating or interpreting for someone else. You MUST be faithful to the person for whom you are interpreting and not interject your own ideas, feelings or opinions into the conversation if you are not part of it.

When you voice or reverse interpret, let the deaf person's concepts flow from you voice the way he is expressing them. Do not add to or take away from what the person you are interpreting for is saying. Be his voice, whether verbal or signed.

People must have faith and confidence in your integrity and your fidelity to what they are saying. Below is the *Code of Professional Conduct* for interpreters in the professional world. It is a good framework in the Christian world as well.

Remember, in church and ministry related interpreting, you may have more flexibility to ensure all parties understand. When interpreting professionally, however, you should adhere to this code as rigidly as possible. Not doing so can open you up to litigation. Here are the basics for the *Code of Professional Conduct* as presented on the web site of the *Registry of Interpreters for the Deaf.*

Code of Professional Conduct
(Adopted July 2005)

The National Association of the Deaf (NAD) and the Registry of Interpreters for the Deaf, Inc. (RID) uphold high standards of professionalism and ethical conduct for interpreters. Embodied in the Code of Professional Conduct (formerly known as the Code of Ethics) are seven tenets setting forth guiding principles, followed by illustrative behaviors.

The tenets of the Code of Professional Conduct are to be viewed holistically and as a guide to professional behavior. The code provides assistance in complying with the code. The guiding principles offer the basis upon which the tenets are articulated. The illustrative behaviors are not exhaustive, but are indicative of the conduct that may either conform to or violate a specific tenet or the code as a whole.

When in doubt, one should refer to the explicit language of the tenet. If further clarification is needed, questions may be directed to the national office of the Registry of Interpreters for the Deaf, Inc.

TENETS

1. Interpreters adhere to standards of confidential communication.

2. Interpreters possess the professional skills and knowledge required for the specific interpreting situation.

3. Interpreters conduct themselves in a manner appropriate to the specific interpreting situation.

4. Interpreters demonstrate respect for consumers.

5. Interpreters demonstrate respect for colleagues, interns and students of the profession.

6. Interpreters maintain ethical business practices.

7. Interpreters engage in professional development.

You can view this Code at:
http://rid.org/ethics/code-of-professional-conduct/

Train Leaders

If you have been in Independent Baptist circles for any length of time, you are aware of the famous saying by Dr. Lee Roberson: *"Everything rises or falls on leadership."*

This truth is greatly demonstrated in the United States Navy. The captain of a ship is solely responsible for the actions of his crew. If they make a mistake that causes loss of life or considerable damage or cost to their ship or the Navy, the captain more than likely will be relieved of command.

He may have had absolutely nothing to do with the mistake personally; however, it is his ship to command and his crew to train. The crew should have been prepared and trained well enough to prevent an incident that was the result of human error.

It is extremely important that you develop leaders, deaf and hearing, who can continue the work. Deaf CAN BE LEADERS. They do not need to depend on the hearing for all of their leadership.

We have many exceptional examples of this in the United States and abroad. Here are some names of successful Deaf leaders in our Independent Baptist circles. This list is NOT exhaustive, only demonstrative. They are listed here alphabetically.

Pastor Fred Adams
Missionary Ray Bradley
Pastor Terry Buchholz
Missionary Nancy Burns
Evangelist John Clark
Pastor Scott Crabtree
Missionary Mary Fuller
Pastor David Hanson
Pastor Bruce Kelly
Pastor Mike Langin

Pastor David Mason
Missionary Vernon Miller
Pastor John Olson
Missionary Maria Podbreski
Missionary Jorge Pozo
Pastor Mike Remington
Pastor Reggie Rempel
Evangelist Ronnie Rice
Evangelist Bill Schutt
Evangelist Allen Snare

As you begin to teach the Deaf, some will respond better than others. Latch onto those who are faithful and excelling, and train and disciple them to be leaders in the Deaf world as missionaries, teachers, pastors, and evangelists. Paul told Timothy:

And the things that thou hast heard of me among many wit-
*nesses, the same commit thou to **faithful men**, who shall be*
able to teach others also. — 2 Timothy 2:2

This mandate applies to the Deaf as well. You will have Deaf that
will be "*apt to teach.*" Help them learn, develop and grow so they
can be used of God. They will be some of your greatest resources
for reaching other Deaf for Christ.

Also, be aware that you are going to have some wonderful Deaf
who will not be able to be primary leaders due to their deafness,
their lack of formal education or their being educated later in life.
This should not stop you from challenging them to be all they can
be for God and using them in ministry.

At *Efata* there are wonderful deaf adults who both would love to
be in full-time Christian service on some mission field or in a
church. Unfortunately, they have emotional and educational issues that have impeded their spiritual growth. However, even
though the church could not commission and send them as missionaries, we can use them in ministry here or to assist other missionaries in accordance with their abilities to serve elsewhere.

Our desire is to use each person to the maximum of his or her
potential in which the Lord has blessed them. At *Efata*, there are
no disposable people. All, both Deaf and hearing, are precious
brothers and sisters in Christ who have value in God's eyes as well
as in ours.

They may not be "*hundred-fold*" or "*five-talent*" leaders. That's
OK. They can do something. Encourage them to serve and par-
ticipate. Help them to realize their potential and exceed it for the
Lord.

For it is God which worketh in you both to will and to do of
his good pleasure. - Philippians 2:13

We must never forget that it is God who is doing the work in us.
He has a plan and He, as the Potter, is molding the clay.

One may not be able to preach but he can be an usher or greeter. He may not be able to teach Sunday school, but he can possibly be a treasurer.

You may have a deaf man that may not be able to be a pastor who builds a great work. However, he could go to an area as a foundational ministry planter, find out where the Deaf are located and teach them sign language and basic Bible principles.

He can help to lay the foundation for a permanent trained pastor or leader to come and continue the work while he goes on to another area and lays the foundation for another new work.

Working to challenge, equip and motivate deaf and hearing workers to reach the Deaf, we **can** make a true difference in their lives all around the world and pierce the *Silence Barrier* that inhibits the Deaf from coming to Christ.

There is no greater joy to this author than to watch the eyes of a deaf person light up with understanding having been enlightened with the Gospel of the Lord Jesus Christ.

That the God of our Lord Jesus Christ, the Father of glory, may give unto you the spirit of wisdom and revelation in the knowledge of him: <u>The eyes of your understanding being enlightened; that ye may know what is the hope of his calling, and what the riches of the glory of his inheritance in the saints,</u> And what is the exceeding greatness of his power to us-ward who believe, according to the working of his mighty power, Which he wrought in Christ, when he raised him from the dead, and set him at his own right hand in the heavenly places,
-Ephesians 1:17-20

4

BUILD
A
TEAM

After these things the Lord appointed other seventy also, and sent them two and two before his face into every city and place, whither he himself would come. Therefore said he unto them, the harvest truly is great, but the labourers are few: pray ye therefore the Lord of the harvest, that he would send forth labourers into his harvest.

- Luke 10:1-2

During the night on a crisp fall evening, the men and boys of the church gathered on the beach to sing, testify, preach and enjoy some good fellowship. It was a cool night by the campfire, the wood crackling and the flames flickering. The retreat was going well and the fellowship continued into the night.

The dawn broke and the waves crashed as the morning was upon them. Most went into the Pacific Ocean to take a swim, some searched for crawfish and sand crabs.

As the haze of the morning broke, the men and boys gathered for one final lesson of the retreat. "If we are ever going to impact the Deaf world for Christ, we must work together." the pastor preached.

As a final object lesson, he tied a rope to the bumper of the pickup truck that was parked on the sand. The pastor asked one of the young men to try to pull the truck. It would not budge. Then one by one, others began to pull. The truck began to move as more men participated. By the time everyone was pulling the rope, the truck moved at the whim of the team that pulled it.

What was impossible for one was easily accomplished by all!

Jesus was an effective team builder. His team of disciples was broken down into groups, or layers. Each layer was a part of the larger one from which it was drawn. The closer the disciple was to Christ, the smaller the group at that level.

There were the three - Peter, James and John, then the twelve, then the seventy, etc.

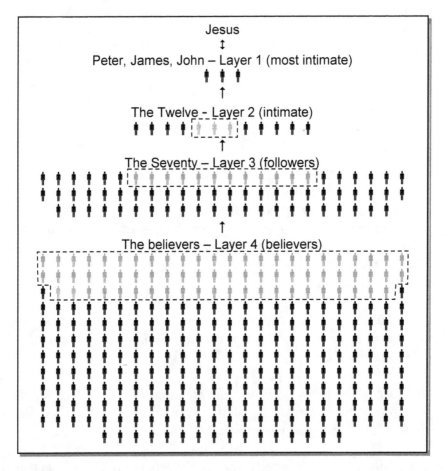

We have enough "Lone Rangers" in the ministry (Really, even the Lone Ranger had Tonto. He was a team player!). The Deaf world needs teamwork if we are going to penetrate the Silent Barrier effectively for Christ. Let's stop worrying about who or what ministry is going to get the credit and let's start building our brother's name so we can build our Saviour's kingdom!

President Harry Truman once said, *"It is amazing what you can accomplish if you do not care who gets the credit."*

President Ronald Regan had a similar saying, *"There's no limit to what a man can do, if he doesn't care who gets the credit."*

Build a team of Deaf and hearing leadership that will be able to help you accomplish the goal of reaching the Deaf. This is especially important on the mission field where you can train and work as a team to reach out together in areas where you alone might never have access.

> *And if one prevail against him, two shall withstand him; and a threefold cord is not quickly broken.*   - Ecclesiastes 4:12

That is solid advice from the Word of God and it is the principle that Jesus taught. He never sent his disciples out alone and neither did the early church. He did not make man to be alone. In fact He specifically said, *"...it is not good that man should be alone."*

One of the greatest assets for a pastor on the mission field (or in any church for that matter) is his team of co-laborers. *Efata Ministries* has grown, not because of a "great" missionary. NO! On the contrary, it has grown because of a GREAT GOD.

God has assembled a dedicated team of servants with goals and a vision to reach Deaf and hearing folks for Christ in a passionate, focused and purposeful way, not through the work of one man but through the work of a **team** of co-laborers who stay busy about the Master's business of reaching the Deaf and hearing for Christ.

As you form your team, do your best to have a good balanced mix of deaf and hearing leaders when possible. Do not favor the hearing over the Deaf. Deaf people are extremely sensitive to this and accuse hearing leaders of favoring the hearing over the deaf all the time. (Most of this is due to the hearing talking more with other hearing as compared to the amount of time spent talking with the Deaf.)

The Deaf need to be sensitive to the hearing world and the natural inclination to enjoy conversing in one's native tongue. Every conversation between hearing people is not gossip about the Deaf just because those talking are not signing.

Those who will be in leadership should be taught to be comfortable with their own lives and not insecure. This insecurity causes many of the problems in the Deaf ministry, just as in the hearing world. Paul said:

I am crucified with Christ: nevertheless I live; yet not I, but Christ liveth in me: and the life which I now live in the flesh I live by the faith of the Son of God, who loved me, and gave himself for me. - Galatians 2:20

Paul also said in Philippians 4:13, *"I can do all things through Christ which strengtheneth me."*

Leaders should know that Christ lives in them, guides them and strengthens them. As long as they are in a right relationship with Christ, the Holy Spirit of God will assist them in their decisions and thus, they need not be insecure.

Younger or newer workers in Deaf ministry should work with older and experienced Deaf leaders and missionaries for at least a few years to gain much-needed experience in Deaf ministry and missions. This is especially needful for hearing people who have little or no prior experience working or living with the Deaf. This advice applies just as well to seasoned missionaries and leaders who are experienced in working in hearing ministries.

Missionaries are notoriously independent and driven people. If they were not, they would not be missionaries. These are good qualities and are a great asset to them on the mission field. This does not negate the need for them to learn and practice the most basic principle of leadership: To be a good leader, you MUST be FIRST a humble follower!

But it shall not be so among you: but whosoever will be great among you, let him be your minister; And whosoever will be chief among you, let him be your servant:
- Matthew 20:26-27

But Jesus called them to him, and saith unto them, Ye know that they which are accounted to rule over the Gentiles exercise lordship over them; and their great ones exercise authority upon them. But so shall it not be among you: but whosoever will be great among you, shall be your minister: And whosoever of you will be the chiefest, shall be servant of all. - Mark 10:42-44

The Deaf ministry is sufficiently different from hearing ministry that it can lead a person to being easily frustrated and discouraged. So many "called" workers with the Deaf are no longer in the Deaf ministry because they were not sufficiently prepared for the unique challenges of this type of ministry. Many do not even last six months.

One way to prevent this frustration and discouragement is to have someone there to help that person grow and learn how to manage and overcome the differences. It is always best for a new servant to have someone who can mentor him with clarity and patience in ministering to the Deaf.

As stated before, just because one knows sign language does not mean that they know the Deaf or their culture. The language is only the beginning. It is only the portal through which we pass to begin our life of learning, loving and then leading the Deaf to Christ.

Set reachable short and long-term goals that you and your team of leaders can focus on, and strive to achieve. Make sure all your team members are on the same page and have the same passion for the goals and mission of your church or ministry. *"Press towards the mark,"* as Paul said, *"for the prize of the high calling which is in Christ Jesus."* Press on together! Go forward!

Always invest in your leadership team, and teach your team to invest in others, both Deaf and hearing. It will be an investment that will produce fruit for eternity.

Your work, your ministry, and your successes will be exponentially greater if you work as a team. There is strength, protection and encouragement in teamwork. Teamwork gets the job done.

We must remember that the most basic team that exists in life and ministry is Christ and you.

In 2 Corinthians 5:18-21 we read the following:

And all things are of God, who hath reconciled us to himself by Jesus Christ, and hath given to us the ministry of reconciliation; To wit, that God was in Christ, reconciling the world unto himself, not imputing their trespasses unto them; and hath committed unto us the word of reconciliation. Now then we are ambassadors for Christ, as though God did beseech you by us: we pray you in Christ's stead, be ye reconciled to God. For he hath made him to be sin for us, who knew no sin; that we might be made the righteousness of God in him.

God chose to partner with His Son to save the world and then allowed us the privilege to be a part of that ministry team by partnering with us and making us His ambassadors. He gave us His ministry, His Word to guide us in how to perform that ministry and His authority to complete that ministry. **Now that is teamwork!**

In Mathew 28:20 Jesus says, "*...lo, I am with you alway, even unto the end of the world.*" What a great comfort and blessing to know we are working as a team with Christ to reach this world, yea the Deaf for Him.

How Does One Build a Team?

Building a team sometimes is a long-term project, especially in Deaf ministry where there are few laborers. Though it may take more time, it is well worth the investment.

Here are some simple guidelines for team building.

- Look for those who have a God-given talent and a desire to work with the Deaf.

- Develop that talent by training, encouraging and helping them to realize their potential in Deaf ministry.

- Work with people who are on the same page and have the same vision as you do. It is hard to move forward if you are philosophically or doctrinally "*unequally yoked.*"

- Develop leaders who will complement your abilities and bring other strengths to the team that may be currently lacking.

- Do not try to build a team of "yes men." You want THINK-ERS and those who will challenge the norm, who can think "out of the box."

- Remember every individual of your team has something to add to the whole, something unique and special. That is the reason God allowed them to be a part of your ministry.

- Build into your team, as Christ did, those leadership lay-ers. Those who have talent, ability and knowledge bring closer to you so that you can train them to train others. Encourage them to build their own teams.

- Build your "brother's name". Praise and encourage your leadership team. Do not take credit. Give it to them, not falsely, but in genuine praise. Thank God often for sending them to work "*in one accord*" with you in the ministry where He has given you the privilege to serve.

- Include and develop both Deaf and hearing leaders.

Pastor Adrian Rogers, longtime pastor of *Bellevue Baptist Church* in Memphis, Tennessee was asked by a young preacher boy once in a meeting how many he was pastoring. His response was enlightening. He told the preachers that when he started he was pastoring 30 men and now (after decades in ministry) he is pastoring 30 men. He told the preachers that those 30 men pastor the rest. At the time he retired and went home to be with the Lord, Pastor Rogers had a congregation of 29,000 members.

You see, he understood that one man cannot pastor a large congregation effectively. One man cannot do it alone. He must train others to lead and share the responsibilities of ministry in the church. A pastor MUST have a team of leaders to effectively build and minister to his church.

Jesus himself did not turn the world upside down. It was His team of disciples that did that. It was because of them working together with one mind and purpose that the Gospel was spread throughout the world in that first generation of the New Testament Church.

Once again, Paul, one of the greatest missionaries, was NEVER alone in ministry. There was always someone to labor encourage or even suffer with him for Christ.

In professional sports, you would never get past training if you could not be a team player. If the sport is a TEAM sport such as, football, basketball, baseball, soccer, volleyball, lacrosse, hockey, etc., you must be a TEAM PLAYER. There is no room for a showoff or a ball hog. You would be benched and removed from the team, no matter how good you are, if you cannot cooperate and work as a team player. This is the same for ministry.

> *Two are better than one; because they have a good reward for their labour. For if they fall, the one will lift up his fellow: but woe to him that is alone when he falleth; for he hath not another to help him up. Again, if two lie together, then they have heat: but how can one be warm alone? And if one prevail against him, two shall withstand him; and a threefold cord is not quickly broken.* - Ecclesiastes 4:9-12

Build a team and watch how your ministry to the Deaf (or any ministry for that matter) grows and strengthens as Deaf and hearing work together for God's glory!

The Team Concept Is a Biblical Philosophy for the Local Church

This author can remember calling pastors while on deputation to request the privilege of presenting the need for missions to the Deaf in Peru with them and their churches. Several times a pastor would say, "I am sorry but we already have a missionary in Peru."

Upon hearing this response, this author normally would ask them if they have a missionary to the **Deaf** in Peru. Invariably the answer was no. However, they still would not see the need and extend an invitation. Other missionaries have faced this same response. It is not unique to missionaries working to reach the Deaf.

One of the leading causes of missionaries leaving the field and returning home is the pressure of being the only ones laboring on their field with no like-minded co-laborers to encourage, help and provided needed fellowship.

This is why Christ taught and practiced the team concept in ministry. He knew the challenges and dangers that would be faced by Christians in this world.

As you read through your Bible you find this team concept everywhere in the New Testament - Paul with Barnabas, Paul with Silas, and Barnabas with Mark. You will NEVER find Paul alone in ministry. Someone ALWAYS was his co-laborer even when he was a prisoner on his way to Rome. (Who do you think wrote the story in the book of Acts? That is correct, the eyewitness that was there with Paul – Luke the physician.)

In addition, you find when Paul struck out alone in going to Corinth he was less effective in ministry and ended up working with his hands making tents. But when relief came by way of Silas and Timothy, he was able to better minister and started a church right next to the synagogue of the Jews and the leader of the synagogue was saved. You can read about this in Acts chapter 18.

You will also see that the Lord Jesus never ministered alone. His first order of business when He began His public ministry was calling out His disciples or His "team". He then reinforced this concept by sending those disciples out "two by two" To minister.

> *And he called unto him the twelve, and began to send them forth by two and two; and gave them power over unclean spirits;* - Mark 6:7

One cannot ignore the team concept in missions for some noble synthetic desire to have ONE missionary in every country.

I would encourage churches to develop missionary teams that can go and work together to reach the lost around the world. Working together, we can accomplish so much more than is possible working alone.

How wonderful it would be if we could train, equip, commission and send teams, of hearing and deaf co-laborers, all around the world to work together to reach Deaf and hearing people for Christ.

The churches and pastors who subscribe to the one missionary per country philosophy of missions are **not** bad people or anti-missionary, no, quite the contrary, most are very missions conscious, they are wonderful, kind and caring pastors; some even visionary. They just have a different missions philosophy.

It is this author's desire that these fine men of God and their churches would prayerfully reconsider their "one missionary – one country" philosophy in light of a renewed review of the Biblical examples and principles of the team missions concept practiced in the Word of God.

"Go ye into all the world" is only one aspect of the missions challenge. One cannot forget about the *"every creature"* mandate, which includes the Deaf and every language and people group of the world no matter the political boundaries.

The wonderful motto, *"United we stand, divided we fall,"* rings true in ministry as well as in patriotism. The Bible has much to say about being united in our faith and service for Christ.

Only let your conversation be as it becometh the Gospel of Christ: that whether I come and see you, or else be absent, I may hear of your affairs, <u>that ye stand fast in one spirit, with one mind striving together for the faith of the Gospel</u>;
- Philippians 1:27

Fulfill ye my joy, that ye be <u>likeminded</u>, having the same love, <u>being of one accord, of one mind</u>.   - Philippians 2:2

Now I beseech you, brethren, by the name of our Lord Jesus Christ, that <u>ye all speak the same thing</u>, and that <u>there be no divisions among you</u>; but that ye <u>be perfectly joined together</u> in the <u>same mind</u> and in the <u>same judgment</u>.
- 1 Corinthians 1:10

For <u>we are labourers together with God</u>: ye are God's husbandry, ye are God's building.   - 1 Corinthians 3:9

We then, <u>as workers together with him</u>, beseech you also that ye receive not the grace of God in vain.
- 2 Corinthians 6:1

Support and build on a team concept of missions. Whether in sending missionaries to the field or whether investing and developing a team on the field. Truly it will produce not only more fruit, but also more fruit that remains. More missionaries will stay on the field and more national leadership will be raised up in effective and impacting world outreach. More "bang" for the mission "buck"!

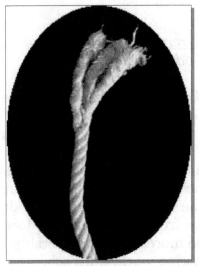

5

METHODS
AND
MODELS

And straightway his ears were opened, and the string of his tongue was loosed, and he spake plain.

- *Mark 7:35*

In 1993 there was a young deaf man who was struggling with an annulled marriage and general issues of life. He was heartbroken that his relationship did not work out and was looking for solutions.

There were no large Deaf ministries nearby and he was attending a church where he was not receiving any help. An assistant pastor at a local Baptist church met him and began working with him. This pastor knew sign language and had worked in a large Deaf ministry for seven years prior to working at this local church. The deaf man grew and was thankful for the attention and help.

The church started a small Deaf ministry and over the years was able to reach a few deaf that lived in the area. The assistant pastor learned a great deal about Deaf ministry during those years. He learned the value of ONE. That assistant pastor is the author of this book.

There are many different types of ministries to the Deaf. Each has value and benefit. There are also differing opinions of what constitutes an official ministry to the Deaf and how one should be organized.

This author has worked in Deaf ministries of all sizes and types and has preached in, as well as attended, countless others both in the United States and around the world.

Good people are successfully ministering to the Deaf the way they believe is effective and best for them as God leads. Just as no two churches are alike, no two Deaf ministries are alike either.

We should always remember that, no matter how many years of ministry and experience we have, we can always learn new and innovative methods of ministry that are Biblical and effective.

This section will begin with the most basic type of ministry to the Deaf and increment from there.

The Personal One-On-One Family/Friend Ministry

This is the type of ministry where a family member or friend works with a single deaf person. They go to church with the deaf person and sit by them and interpret the message for them and/or write down notes of the message for them. There is no other accommodation for the Deaf.

Benefits: Personal relationship and investment in the deaf person by the person who is his or her interpreter/friend. An access to the Gospel that would otherwise not exist.

Limitations: Generally, the person interpreting is a family member or a close friend and they can tend to get "lazy" in the interpretive process and not interpret everything that is going on. If they are writing notes, the deaf person will miss a great deal. The friend or family member cannot pay personal attention to the message, which after a long period of time, may cause him or her to lose interest in serving.

The Interpreter Ministry

This is the church that provides an interpreter for one or all of their services. There are no special classes for the Deaf, only interpreters. The interpreter may be situated in the front of the church or other designated seating area for the Deaf. The interpreter may stand or sit depending on his or her comfort level and the comfort level of the Pastor and people.

Some pastors want to have a Deaf ministry but feel like an interpreter is a distraction away from them or their message. When a ministry is new and having an interpreter is novel to the church, true, it can be distracting for a time. However, without fail, people come up to the interpreter and comment on how they helped the message come alive. The novelty wears off and the church is blessed. The hearing return their attention to the preacher and basically ignore the interpreter.

Benefits: There is more opportunity to reach out to more Deaf. Hearing people see the interpreter thus generating interest in sign language and ministry opportunities with the Deaf.

Limitations: As wonderful as interpreting is, it is still a limited form of communication. The amount of information transmitted is greatly dependent on various factors such as:

- The clarity and speed of the speaker
- The competency of the interpreter
- The complexity of the message
- The quantity of the information presented
- The capacity of the deaf person to assimilate language

The Sunday School Deaf Ministry

This is a common type of Deaf ministry. The church has a separate Sunday school for the Deaf but the services are all interpreted.

Benefits: Allows for teaching the Deaf in their own language and at their own pace. This develops greater learning and training opportunities for the Deaf; allowing the Deaf themselves to become involved in the teaching and ministry process.

Limitations: The same limitations for the *Interpreter Ministry* apply to the *Sunday school Deaf Ministry* as it relates to the preaching time. In addition, space for extra Sunday school classes may not be available.

The Semi-Integrated Deaf Ministry

There are two primary levels of this type of ministry. They both have Sunday school apart from the hearing.

The first level is a non-paid leader or ordained pastor-led ministry that has separate services for the Deaf during one or two of the services during the week. The other services are mainstreamed and interpreted with the hearing.

The second level is a staff pastor to the Deaf, full or part-time (the overwhelming majority are part-time), with his own budget and staff. They also meet apart from the hearing some of the services during the week.

Benefits: All the above plus dedicated staff that specifically focuses on the needs of the Deaf community and membership. Preaching in the language of the Deaf thus provides greater understanding and growth. This type of ministry also helps in fostering greater communion and understanding between Deaf and hearing.

Limitations: Space, budget and available signing staff

The Segregated Deaf Ministry

This is a Deaf ministry where the Deaf have their own leadership in their department and meet completely separate of the hearing but are still part of the main hearing local church. They have some combined activities and services but for the most part, are separate.

Benefits: The Deaf enjoy the benefit of a full-blown ministry for them that is specifically tailored and designed to meet their needs within the local church. There is no need to worry as much about infrastructure as this is provided as a part of the overall ministry of the local church.

Hearing family members can attend with the Deaf or choose to participate in the hearing churches Sunday school programs and classes.

Limitations: Less direct contact with the hearing side of the ministry, which tends to isolationism and distrust in the Deaf ministry regarding the hearing. (Good leadership on both the hearing and Deaf sides can greatly mitigate this limitation.)

Deaf Church

This is a completely separate autonomous local church. It may have a pastor who is deaf or hearing. They meet in their own facilities, rent or use the facilities of other churches.

This type of ministry has the greatest benefit for the Deaf. However, it also has some limitations for the Deaf as a whole and their hearing family members.

Benefits: Ministry totally designed and focused on the needs of the Deaf. All preaching, teaching, evangelism and related ministries are Deaf-centric and thus have the greatest effectiveness for the individual who is deaf.

Limitations: Tends to diminish the care and overlook needs of the hearing family members (The need for skilled hearing voice interpreters and separate classes for the hearing children for example). It is financially difficult to maintain without sufficient membership or external support. (Several deaf churches in America and most on the foreign field depend heavily on monthly mission support.) Also does not allow for the constant exposure of Deaf ministry to the hearing, as it is usually isolated within the Deaf world, which reduces the opportunity to touch hearts of the hearing to volunteer to work with the Deaf.

Each of the above ministries has a place in Christian outreach and ministry to the Deaf. There are many factors that determine what type of ministry one should have or support. Here are some items that help determine this:

Location – Where you are and what the Deaf population is around you. Factors include whether you are near a school for the Deaf or in a large population center with strong Deaf advocacy or small community with very few Deaf and little in the way of services for them.

Level of Deaf population – This relates to the general education and economic level of the Deaf where you serve.

Transportation - Are the Deaf mobile where you are or do they depend on others for their transportation needs?

Level of involvement and commitment in the local church – How involved your pastor and dedicated your people are to serving the Deaf will greatly determine the type of ministry that is most effective where you are.

Skill level of workers – This is a vital area. Do not try to have a Deaf ministry that is beyond the ability of your church to manage realistically and effectively. This can cause a great deal of frustration and hinder your Deaf outreach.

Biases – The preconceived biases or various opinions of pastors and leadership in the Deaf world have a great impact on what type of ministry you will have. Be careful and prayerful about the advice you receive. Consider equally the advice you are given from both deaf and hearing experts in Deaf ministry. Be mindful that many times personal biases influence the counsel that is given.

Finances – Deaf ministries have many of the same financial needs as any other ministry. Thus the type of Deaf ministry you have may be greatly affected by your ability to provide for that ministry.

No matter what your situation, do all you can to reach the Deaf for Christ; they are a part of *"every creature."* Deaf outreach is a tremendous ministry and everyone can have a part in some way or another in reaching a deaf person for Christ.

Choose the ministry type that is right for you in the reality on the ground where you serve. Seek advice and counsel; then do what you believe God would have you to do. Remember, you are God's *"freeman"*! (1 Corinthians 7:22)

Some of the pastors, missionaries and evangelists to the Deaf who have preached at *Efata*.

Deaf Preacher Boys Contest participants
2014

Winner 2014

Winner 2006

Deaf Preacher Boys Contest Participants
2006

EFATA BAPTIST CHURCH

A SPECIAL MINISTRY FOR ALL
LIMA PERU, SOUTH AMERICA

6

SOME
DIFFICULTIES

Now then we are ambassadors for Christ, as though God did beseech you by us: we pray you in Christ's stead, be ye reconciled to God.

- 2 Corinthians 5:20

One day during Sunday school a young deaf woman came and gave a gift to the pastor to the Deaf. It was a beautiful picture. She was thanking him for the wonderful Deaf conference they had just had in the church which was such a blessing to her.

The next Sunday, she did not show up for church. In fact, she never returned. She was fairly new, was growing, had been helpful in finding other Deaf and worked hard to help with the conference. The pastor to the Deaf searched for her to no avail. Finally, one day over a year later, he ran into her. She gave some excuses but it was obvious they were not the reason. After talking further he discovered that she had been offended by one of the visitors from out-of-town during the conference. Because of this, she did not want to return. Her feelings were hurt and she did not allow for reconciliation.

Her gift was a parting one! She was a young Christian damaged by the insensitivity of another but also paralyzed by her inability to get over the offence - to forgive.

Unfortunately, as in most any relationship there will be at times misunderstandings, disagreements and difficulties. The relationships between the Deaf and the hearing are no different.

Deaf and hearing workers in the Deaf community both have positive and, unfortunately, negative issues as it relates to Deaf ministry as a whole. Deaf people often cause much difficulty for those who try to minister to them and, to be sure, hearing people bear their own share of responsibility for failures and problems. Failures in Deaf evangelization and ministry are not one-sided.

Issues Among the Hearing

Many times hearing people who get involved with the Deaf do so because they have a nurturing nature and must have someone to "help." They must feel needed and wanted for their own self-esteem, fulfillment, happiness and satisfaction in life.

In addition, there are hearing people that are controlling and try to manipulate the Deaf because **they** know what is best for them, especially when it comes to their education.

Everyone has an opinion, and his or her opinion is, of course, the "correct" one. However, one shoe does NOT fit all. Each individual is different and has a different set of circumstances in which that individual's needs should be evaluated.

The Deaf do not need another set of parents. They do not need nursemaids in their lives to "help" them. These are relationships that should be avoided. If we are going to be able to successfully minister to the Deaf and bring them to Christ, they need to be respected and partnered with to provide self-motivated, self-initiated solutions for their own lives.

You would be highly upset if someone who was apparently richer, more educated, or of a higher social or political status than you perceive yourself to be, came to you and tried to control your life. You would reject and resist such "help."

Hearing people should try to be understanding of the uniqueness of deafness and of the fears and difficulties that it brings. Though you know that the Deaf need to be self-sufficient, are you helping provide them with the tools, opportunities and training to do just that without creating a "leech" or "welfare dependent" deaf person. Remember it IS a "hearing world" and that puts them at somewhat of a disadvantage.

Hearing people should never believe that they are better, smarter or more competent than deaf people. They should never try to control or manipulate the Deaf. Many well intentioned hearing people make it their life's work to help those "poor little deaf people." Sadly, some do it in a patronizing, controlling and condescending way. This type of "help" is rejected by the Deaf community and rightfully so.

Often one hears of sad stories of interpreters or hearing workers among the Deaf who quit the Deaf ministry because they got their feelings hurt by the Deaf. Worse, many times their feelings are hurt because in their *"hearing know best"* mindset, they cannot accept that a deaf person would reject their help. In their pride, they cannot see that their "lording over" is what is being rejected, not they themselves. If they would truly try to listen, help and work with the Deaf as equals, then they would have much better relationships.

In a large Baptist Church in Florida, the Deaf department was having a contest. It was an attendance related contest and teams were formed. Several men were selected to be team captains. One of them was the Visitation Director at the time and one of his responsibilities was maintaining the attendance records, thus, he was tasked with keeping the count for the contest. To him there was an obvious conflict of interest. He asked not to be a team captain because he knew that it could generate problems. The pastor said that he did not think it would be a problem and wanted him to continue as a captain.

You see, the Pastor had confidence in the Visitation Director's integrity and knew that he would not "cook the books" on the count but would be fair. The Visitation Director was hearing.

Sure enough, one Sunday during the contest, one of the deaf team captains did not like the count and began to complain, criticize and accuse the Visitation Director/captain of counting in favor of his own team. The Visitation Director decided to resign as a team captain, sure that this would satisfy the other. To him, it was the best solution.

Sadly, he was wrong. The deaf captain became even more upset and called him a quitter and dishonest. He was extremely heated and ugly towards the Visitation Director.

The only thing the Visitation Director thought that could have caused such a reaction would be that the deaf captain wanted his team to win over the Visitation Director's team (a Deaf over hearing issue.). Thus, the deaf captain wanted the Visitation Director to continue and not resign as a team captain. He wanted the Visitation director simply to change the count to reflect the deaf captain's version, which the Visitation Director was NOT going to do, as it would have been wrong.

Probably, much of this conflict was the result of the deaf captain's strong spirit of competition, however, he turned it into a "hearing against the Deaf" issue, which it never was.

The Visitation Director was very hurt over this issue because the deaf captain was his friend. It soured their relationship for a long time. The Visitation Director almost quit. His feelings and pride were hurt, as well as his friendship, but quitting was NOT the answer; going forward was!

> *Great peace have they which love thy law: and nothing shall offend them.*   - Psalm 119:165

The Visitation Director wished that he could have done a better job of applying that verse. It took him quite some time to get over the situation and return to a normal relationship with this friend.

It is easy for any of us to be offended, especially with the Deaf. Though some offences are purposeful, many are not. Some are just the result of culture and upbringing and nothing more.

Issues Among the Deaf

By the same token, the Deaf need to realize that they live in a hearing world and that will <u>NEVER</u> change. In eternity all will have the ability to hear. The Bible states in Isaiah 29:18, "*And in that day shall the deaf hear the words of the book, and the eyes of the blind shall see out of obscurity, and out of darkness.*" However, if you are reading this book, that day is not today.

The Deaf need to be thankful and appreciative of every friend, co-worker, family member or ministering person who labors to learn their language and culture. They need to thank God that He has made a way for them to enjoy the riches of eternity. **They just plain need to learn how to be thankful.**

The author can remember one year during some construction at *Efata* a mix of hearing and deaf workers were contracted to help with the construction. There were several salaried employees as well. The unemployment rate during the time was extremely high and it was hard for anyone to find a good job.

One young deaf man had begun coming to the church and worked in construction. To help encourage him the author hired him to help with the construction. He was an excellent worker and everything was fine for a week or so.

Then the trouble began. He began to ask around to see if the Deaf were being paid the same as the hearing. He had a terrible attitude regarding Deaf/hearing relations.

His implication was that *Efata* was not paying the Deaf fairly. This caused a great deal of trouble amongst our workers. They began to question and doubt, then, one by one, they began to complain about their salaries.

What was sad was that one of the deaf men that was complaining was a permanent worker whose salary at the time was higher than most of the hearing workers that were on staff. In fact, the only hearing person that was being paid more was the general contractor on the job. All the contract people, deaf or hearing were being paid the same.

It was explained to the one young deaf man, who was causing all of the trouble, that how much others were paid was none of his business; however, all were being paid fairly. Furthermore, it was clearly explained that *Efata* was a ministry and not a company and was not able to pay what secular contractors were able to pay for any of our workers even though we were paying above what the minimum wage was at the time.

He was not satisfied and continued to imply that *Efata* was paying the hearing more and taking advantage of the Deaf. He was told that he could decide to work or he can go find a better paying job. Nobody was forcing him to work at *Efata*. He was reminded that it was he who asked to work at *Efata*. Unfortunately he continued to argue and thus, the young deaf man was dismissed. Sowing discord among the workers was not an option.

You see the problem was not whether *Efata* was paying unfairly, because they were not. The problem was the Deaf young man had an attitude regarding Deaf/hearing relations. Instead of being thankful that he was given an opportunity to work a good job with free lunch, he was complaining and causing problems.

You might say that there are problems like that among hearing people. It does not seem to be an exclusively deaf/hearing dynamic. This may be very true. The point is that these types of problems are greatly amplified in deaf/hearing - or for that matter - many cross-cultural relationships where language is a problem.

Many hearing people are no longer in the Deaf ministry because of an ungrateful spirit and thanklessness on the part of the Deaf. It is understood that we are not supposed to be working for human accolades; however, there is a Bible command and principle of giving thanks. Saying thank you to someone who has given of himself or herself to invest in another is not a matter of prideful doting, it is a matter of Biblical principle.

Many times the Deaf have an attitude of "victimhood" which breeds a mindset that hearing people "owe" them because of their disability. This is a very unscriptural attitude, and it is very destructive to both the Deaf and hearing and to the interpersonal relationships between them. The Deaf deserve the dignity that God gives all people; however, they do not need to wear their deafness on their shoulders as a chip to be knocked off.

As you work with the Deaf you will find that many have a tremendous amount of interpersonal relationship problems with hearing people. Many deaf individuals perceive themselves to be victims of oppression and control perpetrated upon them by hearing people. Sadly, many of these same deaf individuals do not seem to have a problem with inappropriately taking advantage of a kind and thoughtful hearing person who truly tries to be a real help to them.

The Deaf can and should work and train to support themselves and be successful members of society. They should not expect everything to be done for them. They need to participate in church services and ministry with their lives, talents and resources. <u>The Deaf should strive to become active participants and leaders in life and ministry!</u>

It should be mentioned here that you will often times find that hearing children of deaf adults may exhibit some of the very same interpersonal relationship issues, as their deaf parents. Be mindful of this as you help minister to them as well.

Deaf and Hearing Together

Deaf and hearing people must work together to build bridges for ministry to reach out to the world as God commands. If both cultures submit to the culture of the Bible, giving dignity and honor equally, remembering, "*What is man, that thou art mindful of him?*" and realizing that "the best of men are only men at best," whether deaf or hearing, then we will have success and see fruitful ministry taking place among the Deaf and their families.

A young man in a church for the Deaf went off to Bible college. After a time, he was having problems with working with the Deaf. He told his pastor that he was tired and fed up with such a hard ministry. He mentioned that it was much easier to work with the hearing in the church and community than with the Deaf.

His pastor told him to hang in there and remember that no ministry is easy. What makes the Deaf ministry so hard is the same thing that makes it so rewarding – the overcoming of obstacles and challenges as we *"fight the good fight of faith."* When we see the Deaf respond and grow, it makes it worth it all.

This young man grew up around the Deaf. He has family who are Deaf serving in full-time Christian service. He has worked in ministry with the Deaf for several years. Yet, under the extra pressures of Bible college and ministry, the uniqueness of Deaf ministry began to wear him down. He no longer works with the Deaf.

Both Deaf and hearing need to remember one fundamental truth in ministry: it is not about Deaf, it is not about hearing, it is not about us. **It is about God**. It is about loving what God loves. The Bible says, *"For God so loved the world..."* If God thought it was important enough to create deaf people, then surely it is important enough to Him that we minister to them, no matter what the difficulties may be.

We do not let the difficulties of reaching the Muslim world for Christ stop us from trying. Equally, we should not let the difficulties of the Deaf world stop us from ministering there either.

One of the highest forms of praise is emulation. The best way we can emulate our Heavenly Father is to love what HE loves! He loves the hearing AND the Deaf!

There Will Be Discouragements

Please remember, we all get discouraged at times in ministry. The Deaf ministry is a great catalyst for discouragement; the Deaf you have loved and invested in get offended and leave, the deaf children you have cared for in the school and home grow up only to abandon the faith-drawn in by the secular would and its trappings and the leaders you have trained and faithfully labored with fall into sin and reject the biblical restoration process.

The best and most famous preachers of old had times of great depression. Charles Spurgeon, that great prince of preachers often struggled with depression. Many preachers are overcome and leave the ministry or worse. It is a real problem. This author can list many names of former Deaf preachers and leaders who are nowhere to be found today.

The Bibles states in Proverbs 13:12, "*Hope deferred maketh the heart sick...*". Our hearts can become very sick over our perceived lack of success in Deaf ministry. That is Biblical depression. However, the <u>verse</u> continues on to say, "*but when the desire cometh, it is a tree of life.*" What an encouragement! That is revival of the heart.

When we realize that it is God that is responsible for the results, we can rest and rejoice in what He is doing through our faithfulness. Do not let the fear of man bring a snare to you! Just be faithful to God's call in your life and do not give in to the temptation of Satan to quit.

> *Moreover it is required in stewards, <u>that a man be found faithful</u>.*   -1 Corinthians 4:2

> *Who then is Paul, and who is Apollos, but ministers by whom ye believed, even as the Lord gave to every man? I have planted, Apollos watered; but <u>God gave the increase</u>. So then neither is he that planteth any thing, neither he that watereth; but <u>God that giveth the increase</u>.*   -1 Corinthians 3:5-7

One of the most powerful booklets I have ever read regarding success in ministry is called *Obsessed with Success* by Dr. Jim Binney. He quotes in his booklet a quotation from William H. Cook from his book *Success Motivation and the Scriptures* which states:

> *Success is the continuing achievement of being the person god wants me to be, and the continuing achievement of establish goals God helps me set.*

Dr. Binney Further states:

Success is the process (not a product) of "...always abounding in the work of the Lord." It is an open ended process of faithfulness to God's divine orders for you and you alone. It is not a driving obsession to draw attention to self, to ascend a "throne," wearing a crown of man's making rather it is the obsession of which Paul speaks.
Whether therefore ye eat or drink or whatsoever ye do, do all to the glory of God (1 Corinthians 10:31)

If we keep our expectations for successful Deaf ministry (or any ministry for that matter) firmly grounded in the Word of God, it will help us overcome the depression that comes will unrealized expectations of success that are self-developed instead of biblically developed.

Jesus loves the little children,
All the children of the world.
Hearing, seeing, yes, it's true,
The Deaf and blind, He loves them too.
Jesus loves the little children of the world.

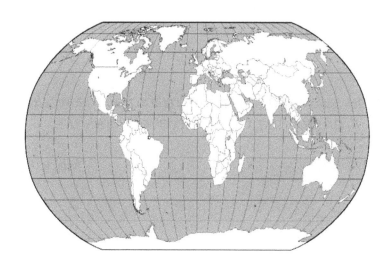

7

GOING
GLOBAL

(WORLD WIDE DEAF MISSIONS)

And he said unto them, Go ye into all the world, and preach the Gospel to every creature.

- Mark 16:15

—

As the young couple stepped off the bus, they were excited and intimidated by what lay ahead. They were from another country and this was the first time they had ever ventured outside of theirs; add to this they were fairly newly-weds. However, they knew that God had called them to work with the Deaf though they did not know how.

For the next six months, they would train and work in various areas of Deaf ministry in Lima, Peru, so they could return to their home in Caracas, Vene-zuela to begin a new ministry for the Deaf. It was an exciting and challenging time for them, living in a strange country, adjusting to a new culture and all of the challenges of being newly married.

They would work hard and learn all they could in those short six months. They would develop lasting relationships and friendships with the workers and the Deaf children they would work with during that time.

When the time came, they returned to Venezuela, and with their new knowledge of Deaf and Deaf ministry, Rafael and Erika Ramirez began a work that has now become the largest Independent Baptist Deaf ministry in Venezuela.

Thus began the global training outreach of Efata Ministries.

In every corner of the world and in every country on the earth there are deaf people who need to know the Gospel. We have a mandate from the Lord Jesus Christ to reach this population that lives in silence. *"Every creature"* means just that. Everyone should be afforded the opportunity to make a decision for Christ.

George Otis once said that *"Jesus will judge us not only for what we did, but also for what we could have done and didn't."* In the area of Deaf missions, there is a lot more that could be done that is not. We CAN do more and we MUST.

If we are going to have an effect on New Testament Worldwide Deaf missions, we need to change our thinking about the significance and importance of Deaf outreach.

This raises the question: What is the worth of a soul? You would say that there is no realistic expense too great for reaching a lost soul for Christ. However, when that lost soul is housed in a deaf body, somehow, the cost analysis changes. One supposedly does not get as big a "bang for their buck" when working with deaf people.

Is Deaf ministry hard? Yes! Is it frustrating? Yes! Is it costly in comparison to the same investment in hearing ministry? Yes! Therefore, **SO WHAT**? Is it worth the investment? YES! You cannot put a price on a soul and the soul of a deaf person is a "pearl of great price."

To illustrate this for you, how many people in this world spend two, three, four or even ten times the money to buy a high-end "writing instrument" (pen or mechanical pencil). They say, "I deserve the best and want it to last." (They also want to impress their friends with the quality and expense of the item bought.) They could have bought several 20 packs of standard medium or fine point pens in assorted colors for the price of that one writing instrument.

However, when it comes to ministry to the Deaf, they cannot see investing money in one Deaf soul when it could be invested in 10 or 20 hearing people. We spare no expense for ONE nice trinket but ONE Deaf soul does not have the same value.

The problem may lie in a great chasm of forgetfulness as to where the funds for ministry really come from. They come from GOD through the hands of HIS people. God has enough funds for the 20 hearing people as well as the one deaf person.

Here is another analogy. We will invest tens of thousands of dollars in a home remodeling project just to keep our homes up-to-date and in style with the Jones' home. How sad when we could be spending that same amount of money helping others with their houses.

Just trying to give a little perspective to the issue, as there is nothing wrong with having a nice pen or a modern home. By the same token, there is nothing wrong with investing in the lives of the Deaf with our best and brightest God-called young people and our financial resources.

A new missionary training to work with the Deaf was sitting in the office of his pastor one day and they were talking about the missionary's desires and future work among the Deaf. As they talked, the missionary began to share a story with the pastor about a conversation he had with an American missionary working in Argentina.

He had gone to this missionary to share his burden and calling. When the missionary heard it, he was not much of an encouragement. The missionary in essence said to him, "Why do you want to waste your time and talent working with the Deaf? It is not a very cost effective ministry. You will see so little results and the results will not be worth the effort."

The new missionary and his wife were both professionals in the secular world of social work. Both had prestigious degrees and professions. However, they had something more - a burning desire from God to reach the Deaf in Argentina. It is a wide-open mission field among their people.

This couple sold everything they had, left good jobs and moved to Peru for two years to train to reach the Deaf. They willingly left all to serve the Lord.

It is a sad and dangerous attitude, though not uncommon among results-oriented missionaries and preachers who base their self-esteem and ministry success on the quantity of the count and not the faithfulness to the work of the Lord.

If the Lord Jesus Christ could go out of his way and expend time, money and talent to heal one deaf man in Mark chapter 7, can we not do the same? YES!

Surely that missionary was glad that someone saw the value of **ONE** in him. Why would he not want that opportunity for a deaf person in Argentina whom he is not going to reach?

We love hearing the song *"The Value of One"* sung in our mission conferences. It touches our hearts and brings tears to our eyes; but do we really desire to live its reality in our ministry and mission philosophies?

How to Reach the Deaf Globally

There are many methods for reaching hearing folks that are effective and successful. Here are some methods of ministry for hearing people that generally have a diminished or limited impact on Deaf ministry:

- Radio or any other ministry that depends specifically on one's ability to hear, such as audio podcasting.

- Correspondence ministries - The impact of these methods depend greatly on the language capacity of the Deaf. We desire to place a Bible in their hands, however, for most it will take a great deal of time to help them understand what they are reading. Just giving a tract, Bible or lesson will be ineffective apart from the language skills needed to benefit from them.

- Television ministries (Limited benefit with programs that have simultaneous interpreting or closed captioning)

Each of the above depends greatly on the education and access level of the Deaf to benefit from them. What good is a Bible, tract or lesson if the deaf person cannot read it? Do they get extra dispensations of mercy at the Great White Throne because they were in possession of such treasures? It is wonderful to get a Bible into the hands of a deaf person. However, it is important to educate them in how to use that Bible. Remember the Ethiopian Eunuch:

And Philip ran thither to him, and heard him read the prophet Esaias, and said, Understandest thou what thou readest? And he said, How can I, except some man should guide me? And he desired Philip that he would come up and sit with him.   *- Acts 8:30-31*

These methods mentioned above can be used to educate hearing people and family members of deaf people about your ministry and presence. This will allow the hearing to help the Deaf find you and thus they can be used in indirect ways to reach the Deaf.

The most effective way to reach the Deaf, as with the hearing, is to reach them one by one in personal ministry. Where mass media ministry can be very successful among the hearing, it is only minimally effective at best among the Deaf.

NO MATTER WHAT, THE DEAF NEED A PREACHER!

*For whosoever shall call upon the name of the Lord shall be saved. How then shall they call on him in whom they have not believed? and how shall they believe in him **of whom they have not heard?** and **how shall they hear without a preacher**? And how shall they preach, except they be sent? as it is written, How beautiful are the feet **(hands)** of them that preach the Gospel of peace, and bring glad tidings of good things!*   *- Romans 10:13-15*

Things to Consider When Choosing a Ministry Location for the Deaf (These are specific to Deaf ministry apart from what would be normal for any new missionary.)

- Is there an already established form of sign language for that country?

- If so, how broad or limited is that language and will you need to develop the Christian signs for the language?

- How advanced is the state education system for the Deaf?

- Does the state provide institutions of higher learning for the Deaf and teachers who teach the Deaf?

- Based on the above, will you need to start a school for the Deaf?

- What are the societal norms, customs and attitudes towards the Deaf?

- As a result of the above, what is the image the Deaf have of themselves?

- What kind of attitudes and relationships exist between the Deaf and their families?

- Is there a social aid system in place to care for the needs of orphaned, abused or abandoned deaf children?

- Will you need to start an orphanage for the Deaf?

- Is there a hearing church that you can work with as you begin ministry or are you going to have to strike out completely on your own?

- Are there already established clubs for the Deaf, associations or ministries from which you can glean?

These are some of the basic questions you will need to ask yourself regarding the country and location that God has called you to minister.

The most important first step, once the country and location where you will minister is decided, is to learn all you can about the country, the community and the Deaf.

No matter what country that you are working in, the best choice for reaching the Deaf is to find where the Deaf have the highest population concentration and begin there. Generally speaking, wherever the greatest population of Deaf is, the wider the variety of Deaf you will have to work with in terms of education and ability.

Of course, during this process you will begin to develop relationships with the hearing people surrounding the lives of the Deaf, as well as others that you will inspire to work with the Deaf. This is not necessarily a short-term process. If you are looking for instant success and instant sustainable crowds of Deaf, your goals are not realistically focused.

Remember, we are not the "Great White Hope" for the Deaf. We are servants and messengers of the great hope of the Gospel and our great God and Saviour, Jesus Christ.

Ways of Finding the Deaf

These methods of finding the Deaf on the foreign mission field are very similar to those we briefly mentioned in Chapter Three with a few differences. Each country is different and some methods will be more appropriate in westernized countries and others more effective in third world countries.

Word of mouth -Tell people what you are doing and why you are there in their country. You will meet people who know of some deaf person living near them. You can use that as an access point. Speak to cab drivers as you travel. They meet many people as they work during the day. Of course in countries where it is illegal to preach or proselytize, you must be very careful.

Phone Book - Look in the local listings for any deaf organizations, government or private that you can contact for information. This can be a challenge. Yellow Pages in foreign countries are laid out with a logic based on the language and customs of that country. It is not always easy to find what you are looking for if you approach their Yellow Pages with a North American mindset and logic.

Police & other emergency services – If you can develop a relationship with them, they can be very helpful. Many times the police have constant contact with delinquent Deaf because they have been ignored or left to their own by their families, and the street is all they really know. You must be careful with these Deaf. however, the good news that you bring them about God and His wonderful salvation in Christ is just the "fix" they need to change their lives.

Other churches, missionaries, pastors – Let other churches know you are there to minister to the Deaf. Have them let you know if they have any deaf people or family members with deaf relatives in their congregations or sphere of influence that they would be willing to help you reach for Christ.

Other Deaf – The most effective way in finding deaf people is through other deaf people. The Deaf community is very small and tight. If you can win some of the key players in the Deaf community, you will be able to reach many deaf people this way.

Door to door canvas – This is effective as you knock on doors and ask if there are any deaf people in the area that the neighbors know about. Please note, many times the family will be embarrassed that they have a deaf child. They will look at it as a curse from God depending on their religious world-view.

One day while out on visitation, some members of our church went to a house where we thought a deaf young person was living. When they arrived at the house, the mother let them in. They explained that they were looking for deaf people to help and the mother said that there was no one that lived there that was deaf.

The visitors noticed that there was a young man sitting on the couch that was watching this conversation but said nothing. The way he was watching and not reacting caught their attention and one of the visitors went to him to greet him and ask his name.

When there was not response, the visitor began to sign and the young man lit up. *He was deaf.*

The mother was so embarrassed about her son's deafness, that she was willing to lie to the visitors with her deaf son present in the room. Do not judge her harshly as she comes from a different culture and religious background. These differences helped to create the mindset upon which her actions and reactions were based. She was not a Christian. This same story has been reported countless times by missionaries in different countries.

Media inquiries and announcements – Advertise and announce with public service announcements. Many times, these are free to the public.

Governmental agencies – Especially focus on the Ministry of Education, local school districts and social service agencies. Also speak with human service agencies.

Non-Governmental Agencies – There are a host of non-governmental philanthropic agencies in foreign countries that may have social assistance programs that target the disadvantaged and disabled. They may be able to help you in locating the Deaf.

Malls and public gathering areas – Deaf love to congregate and fellowship. They usually have specific places and times when they meet. Try to find these places and times and show up. Sadly, the Deaf participate in many un-Christian activities such as bar hopping, going to the disco and gambling establishments. They love Bingo. Be mindful of your testimony as you seek the Deaf near these types of locations.

Street venders and beggars – Many Deaf sell trinkets or sign language ABC cards on the street or in shopping areas, airports and places where there are many people. Be observant of this. Unfortunately, many deaf people who beg or panhandle are working for someone else who is exploiting them.

Though cultures and languages are different, basic Bible ministry is the same. Practice sound Biblical missions principles and apply them to Deaf missions as well. Then learn and apply the unique challenges to reaching the Deaf. Our ultimate goal is to glorify God by faith in His ability to guide us in the right paths to fulfill His will.

You Have Found a Deaf Person – What's Next?

You want to develop relationships as soon as possible with deaf people so you can learn from them their culture, attitudes, language and manner of life. As you develop these relationships, you will begin to see Deaf saved and you can disciple them and begin to develop your ministry team among the national Deaf.

Again, ministry is about relationships. Build authentic relationships with the Deaf that you meet. This process will allow you to evaluate the language and education level of the deaf people with whom you are working, which in turn will guide you to the most effective way to reach them for Christ.

In addition, they will become your teacher in their language and its use and in the culture of the Deaf where they live. Deaf people love to teach their language to new friends.

Rafael, the missionary to the Deaf in Venezuela, had a Deaf friend that worked for the government at the ministry of health. He is well educated and has a very good government job.

Rafael became interested in ministry to the Deaf through the relationship and friendship that he developed with this Deaf man. He was the one who taught him Venezuelan Sign Language and introduced him to the Deaf community and culture in Venezuela. Every day at lunchtime, a group of Deaf who worked in that area would meet in the courtyard for fellowship. The Lord used that relationship to spark a fire for the Deaf ministry in Rafael's heart.

Build relationships with the Deaf and you will reap the dividends later. There are no five-minute salvation decisions with the Deaf. (In my opinion, there are not too many with hearing folk either.)

Groundwork must be laid to successfully minister and open the eyes of understanding for the Deaf to receive Christ as Saviour. It takes time to do this. Be prepared to make the time.

A road that is paved before the groundwork or foundation is finished soon becomes rough to drive on as it becomes laden with potholes. If not repaired, the road will eventually become impassible and can damage those vehicles that travel thereon.

Ministry is the same way. Without a good foundation of relationships, it will become hard and could eventually damage those to whom we seek to minister, as well as those who are ministering.

Do Not Be Offended If You Are Not Initially Accepted.

Just because you know or are learning sign language does not mean that the Deaf are going to flock to your side. As stated before, the Deaf are very cautious of new hearing people entering their silent world.

When Rafael and Ericka returned to Venezuela to begin ministering to the Deaf, they were not accepted right away. He tells of a humorous story that happened to him one day while he was out visiting the Deaf. He was so excited when he came upon a group of deaf people and began talking to them. After a few minutes one of the deaf ladies there asked if he was deaf and he said no that he was hearing.

That deaf lady completely changed her attitude towards him and with a scowl on her face turned her back to him and began talking with the other Deaf that were there completely ignoring him.

Manuel, a missionary to the Deaf in Argentina, trained at *Efata* shared a similar story. During an Anniversary Sunday at *Efata* he noticed a group of visiting Deaf. He went over and began talking with them.

During the conversation, which was very cordial, his son Renzo came and asked him a question. Manuel quickly answered his son with his voice and not his signs.

One of the deaf ladies present in the conversation saw this and with dismay in her expressions asked if he was hearing or deaf. Manuel told her that he was hearing. When he told her this, with indignation she said "you're a liar!" "You lied to me. You told me you were Deaf!"

Manuel was taken aback. He never once told her that he was deaf or hearing for that matter. It was not a part of the conversation. She simply assumed that he was deaf because he came up to her group and began conversing in sign language without moving his lips or talking.

There are some deaf people who will initially reject your inclusion in their culture just because you are hearing. It will take time and patience to build relationships with those deaf people. It is not impossible, just more of a challenge.

Let this challenge motivate you to work harder and not give up. Cross cultural challenges are to be bridged and overcome with patience and wisdom. Do not let them diminish your zeal and desire to minister and reach out to the Deaf world.

Rafael struggled for six months before realizing even a hint of fruit in Deaf ministry. He would invite the Deaf to church and when a deaf person would visit and see that he or she was the only deaf person present, they would not come back.

One day Rafael found one deaf man who knew no signs and was isolated from both the deaf and hearing worlds. He befriended him and began to teach him sign language. This young man blossomed. He received Christ as his Savior and became a faithful member at their church.

Then, with one faithful deaf man, other deaf began to come to church and the ministry grew from there. Those first six months were a great struggle to Rafael and his wife. He expressed to this author that were it not for his training at *Efata,* he would have "thrown in the towel" before his first year of ministry with the deaf was over. His time at *Efata* had prepared him for many of the struggles and surprises that Deaf culture has to offer that are different than normal hearing ministry. His training helped him during those difficult times. He was able to see deaf men as leaders and pastors and deaf ladies serving the Lord. Rafael knew it could be done because he saw that it was (and is) being done!

At times it is difficult to gauge if one is having a life changing effect in ministry with the Deaf. If one is patient and dependent on God's sustaining and motivating power found in His Word, one can rest in the increase that God will give as one plants and another waters. Remember, we are not to judge our success or failure by the numbers we produce, that is God's business. Success in ministry comes through humble submission to the Lord and in laboring for Him.

Rafael said it was extremely frustrating to see a deaf person that one has trained, discipled and invested in for months, turn right around and live exactly opposite of all that they were taught. However, knowing that the Deaf can and do succeed gives him strength to continue serving in this vital ministry.

The Great Global Need

But ye shall receive power, after that the Holy Ghost is come upon you: and ye shall be witnesses unto me both in Jerusalem, and in all Judaea, and in Samaria, and unto the uttermost part of the earth. - Acts 1:8

Going global in Deaf missions is mandated by the Word of God. In the above verse we can see that Jesus Christ told his disciples to go into their own city (Jerusalem), their regional area (Judea), their neighboring regions (Samaria) and the rest of the World (uttermost part of the earth) **All AT THE SAME TIME!**

One region was not to be neglected over the other. A local church should not abandon church planting efforts in their own area and neighboring regions so as to be fully engaged in world missions.

All should be done in a balanced simultaneous way. An application could be made here as well regarding people groups: *Jerusalem* – your family, *Judea* – your friends and neighbors, *Samaria* – Your culture and language group, *Uttermost parts of the Earth* – Other culture and language groups such as the Deaf

There are literally millions of Deaf and hard-of-hearing people in the world today with little to no access to the Gospel. The following web links have information on Deaf populations in the United States and other countries around the world.

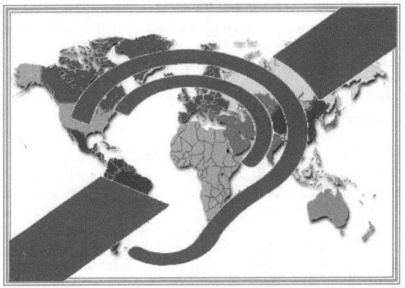

Gallaudet University Library:

http://libguides.gallaudet.edu/deaf_statistics

Deaf World Ministries:

http://www.deafworldministries.com/stats.html

It is virtually impossible to get a true and accurate count of the deaf/hard-of-hearing populations of the world. However, these sites will at least give you an honest reference upon which one can better understand the need. Frankly, no one truly knows how many deaf and hard-of-hearing people live behind the *silent Window*.

Train National Leadership

If we are ever going to reach this world for Christ, whether the hearing world or the Deaf world, we MUST train and develop national leadership.

Americans do not have the corner on the spiritual market. The same Holy Spirit that calls, leads and uses American national missionaries is the same Holy Spirit that calls, leads and uses national missionaries from any country. American missionaries need to train and equip the men and women that God places in their care and then *LET THEM GO!*

As American missionary effort and even dollars are steadily declining, the need to train and equip national leaders becomes even more pronounced.

Paul said this about the Church at Rome:

> *First, I thank my God through Jesus Christ for you all, that your faith is spoken of throughout the whole world.*
> - Romans 1:8

How is it that the world was turned upside down? How is it that the Church at Rome's faith was spoken of throughout the whole world? Simply put, it was the SENDING OUT of national missionaries from the local church that was founded in Rome.

This church was not located in Jerusalem or Antioch. It was in Rome, in Italy. The Church at Rome was such a fantastic and impacting global ministry that Paul, one of the greatest missionaries ever, wanted to go there as soon as he could so that he could have fruit among them. (Romans 1:10-13)

There were no printed tracts, handbills or revival posters. There were no radio, television, satellite or internet pod-casts. There was no Bible distribution or printing ministry. There were no cars, planes, trains or other modern transportation methods to carry the Roman missionaries to the "uttermost parts" of the world.

What the Church at Rome did, they did by foot, hoof or boat. They had no ATMs, Western Unions or wire transfers. The Church at Rome had NOTHING in comparison to what modern-day missionaries have at their disposal to reach the world.

What the Church at Rome DID have was the power of the Holy Spirit, the passion of the cross and the pioneering spirit to propagate the Gospel to every land.

It is not known who started the Church at Rome. Whoever it was did a wonderful job training the Roman gentiles (the nationals) to reach the world.

The more national missionaries, pastors, leaders and faithful serving church members that we train, send out and encourage, the greater the impact will be in reaching the lost.

Paul told Timothy:

> *And the things that thou hast heard of me among many witnesses, the same <u>commit thou to faithful men, who shall be able to teach others also</u>.*   — 2 Timothy 2:2

Once again, that is what we need to do if we are going to reach the Deaf for Christ around the world. We need to seek out and teach *"faithful men who will be able to teach others also."*

In this book you will notice several times that emphasis is placed on the need for men in Deaf ministry. This author cannot stress this need more strongly. The Church of Jesus Christ MUST seek out and encourage ***men*** who are *apt* and *faithful* who can enter this vast and needy mission field around the World – the mission field of the Deaf.

An American missionary to the Deaf cannot afford to be focused solely on building his own church on the mission field. He needs to be focused on developing national leadership in already existing churches and he needs to break ground in new areas with a pioneering spirit.

The Bible says about the first century Church, they turned the world upside down and the Gospel spread throughout the whole world.

> *And when they found them not, they drew Jason and certain brethren unto the rulers of the city, crying, <u>These that have turned the world upside down are come hither also</u>;*
>
> — Acts 17:6

> *Which is come unto you, <u>as it is in all the world</u>; and bringeth forth fruit, as it doth also in you, since the day ye heard of it, and knew the grace of God in truth:*
>
> — Colossians 1:6

> *But I say, Have they not heard? <u>Yes verily, their sound went into all the earth</u>, and their words unto the ends of the world.*
>
> — Romans 10:18

The New Testament Church turned the world upside down and filled it with their doctrine by training the national people wherever they went. They did not depend on those first disciples and apostles to do all the work.

With this in mind, we should not wait and depend solely on American missionary effort and help to get the job done. Reaching this world is the responsibility of ALL Christians no matter where they are from or language they speak.

This author can remember one day, while he was attending a meeting with several national pastors and missionaries, one of the directors of the mission organization that was sponsoring the nationals was explaining the details to them regarding the mission conference they would be attending.

The Director was a former pastor and had at that time been involved for many years with working with national pastors and missionaries. He loved them and they loved him. He has given his heart to the work of supporting national men and has been very successful in doing so.

However, he made a statement that this author will never forget. While he was discussing the time limits for their messages he made this statement: "Americans have heard the greatest preachers in the world, you do not have anything new to preach to them. Just give them your burden."

This author has never forgotten those words to this day. As tremendous a man of God that preacher is, as caring and respectful of national missionaries he is and as often as he has traveled abroad and seen some of the tremendous works on the mission field – started and growing completely by national pastors; he still had an "America is the Best" attitude and mindset.

Those dear national men smiled and politely accepted the admonition. (Of course they would, their funding source depended on it. Who controls the purse strings controls the person; a sad but true reality for most.) The problem for this author was and still is, HE was WRONG! Some of the greatest preaching I have ever heard in my life came from national pastors. I would put some of them on an equal footing with any of America's finest.

TRAIN, EQUIP, SUPPORT and SEND the national people you go to the mission field to SERVE! That is how we will *Turn the world upside down* in OUR GENERATION!

Americans and nationals
working together to
turn the world upside down¡

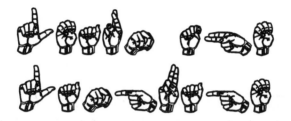

8

LEARN
THE
LANGUAGE

And the Gileadites took the passages of Jordan before the Ephraimites: and it was so, that when those Ephraimites which were escaped said, Let me go over; that the men of Gilead said unto him, Art thou an Ephraimite? If he said, Nay; Then said they unto him, Say now Shibboleth: and he said Sibboleth: for he could not frame to pronounce it right. Then they took him, and slew him at the passages of Jordan: and there fell at that time of the Ephraimites forty and two thousand.

- Judges 12:5-6

Manuel, a tall professional man from Argentina rose to the platform to begin his message. He had worked for the government as a degreed and licensed professional in social work. His wife Paola was a professional interpreter for the Deaf. They were now in Peru training to work with the Deaf in Biblical ministry. Manuel had limited knowledge of sign language when he came to Efata and during several months of total immersion he was ready for training in preaching in sign language.

His message was a good one but his sign language lacking; both in the formation and use. He was being videoed for training and the critique began. "Wow pastor, I did horribly today." he lamented, as we watched the video. We analyzed the strong and weak points correcting his grammar and use. A few weeks later the results were markedly better. Language learning was taking place and a new missionary was being formed to work with the Deaf in Argentina.

The most important investment in ministry as it relates to missions is the investment you will make to learn the native language of the country and people group with whom you will be working. Not only the sign language but also the SPOKEN language **_BEFORE_** you set out to begin major ministry! It will pay you dividends later on.

Too many missionaries, including this author, have been frustrated or hindered in ministry due to poor language development and training. You will be extremely grateful to those who have pushed you to excel in language.

Not only do you want to learn the language, but also you want to learn the idiomatic expressions and colloquialisms - informal words or phrases that are more common in conversation than in formal speech or writing.

In our zeal to go to work and see folks saved, we at times look for short cuts to success in ministry. Frankly, there are none. The same applies to language learning. Some may have an excellent aptitude for languages while others may not. No matter how adept you are in language learning, it is extremely important to obtain competence no matter how long it will take. Patience IS a virtue in language development and learning. Many senior missionaries on the field have said that you never stop learning when it comes to language however you CAN be competent and confident in the languages you learn.

Remember, God knew your aptitude for language learning when He called you to your field of service. **He knows** how long it is going to take and what it is going to cost you to succeed, STAY AT IT! He chose YOU for a reason, which does not have to be obvious to you or anybody else at the time.

Being confident of this very thing, that he which hath begun a good work in you will perform it until the day of Jesus Christ: - Philippians 1:6

Some missionaries spend years learning and developing written languages for countries, tribes and peoples who have no written language, and hence, no Word of God in their spoken language.

This process is meticulous and laborious, however, their patience and dedication have led to whole villages and tribes being saved and having the written Word of God available to them.

On the other hand, there are places where missionaries went in and tried to use a "bridge" language – one that they knew, but was only a second language to the native people. This resulted in many years of ineffective ministry. It took years for the missionaries who finally learned the language to reach these people effectively with the Gospel. The missionaries were greatly surprised when, as they truly learned the native language and began to preach and teach in it, they found that the native people were NOT saved. They had just added the rituals and activities of this new "white man's religion" to their own superstitious ways.

Language Learning as it Relates to Deaf Ministry

If you are a hearing person working with the Deaf, you must not focus on the sign language to the expense of the spoken language in the country where you will minister as a missionary.

If you are a deaf person working with the Deaf, you cannot ignore the written or spoken language of the country where you will work. It is IMPERATIVE that you be able to effectively communicate. Knowing only the sign language and not the spoken or written language of the people group you are serving will greatly hinder your ministry.

You will be teaching deaf people how to read, write and reason. You will need spoken/written language to be able to understand their language so you can provide materials and lessons for those you will teach.

One of the greatest mistakes of this author in preparation for ministry to the Deaf in Peru was NOT learning the spoken Spanish language well, before beginning full-time ministry in Peru. There was every good intention to do so; however, becoming too involved in the work caused the development of many bad language habits. Going to another city or place to focus on language learning is what should have been done initially.

The thinking was that a competence in American and Peruvian Sign Languages could be used as a basis for immediate ministry with the Deaf in Peru. The sign language would in essence become a bridge to helping learn the spoken language. The exact opposite was true. It was a hindrance to this author's language learning. While it helped in learning some Spanish vocabulary, it was counterproductive in helping with the structure of the spoken language.

For hearing people, think about the way you perceive tourists who come to the United States from another country. Many times they only have a rudimentary knowledge of English. If you are like most, you thought that the person who was talking was somewhat ignorant. However, you may have been talking with a person who holds a PHD, a person who had two or three times the higher education that you have. Do not feel bad, most people think that way and it has been the subject of many jokes and comedy routines.

Though this author can fluently converse with a Spanish speaker, it becomes instantly clear that he is a "gringo" and an expert in *Spanglish*. This author has added many "new" words to the *Spanglish* lexicon. Here are a couple of those words just for fun:

- *imprubar* – To improve (Spanish - mejorar)
- *Fellowshipe* – Fellowship (Spanish - compañerismo)

For the Deaf, think about how you look at a person who is just learning sign language but *thinks* they are good. Deaf people do not generally sign to hearing people the way they do to other native signers. The Deaf have to "dumb down" their language for the hearing so the hearing can understand them. As the hearing person learns the structure, intricacies and expressions of sign language, the Deaf signer will begin to speak to them as they do to other Deaf.

Sign Language

Sign language is not universal. In fact, it is quite different in many countries. Many hearing people seem to be surprised by this. It is context, concepts and culture that determines meanings. All three play a major role in language development. Here is an illustration that should help:

*Example: Before you walk out with him secure your bonnet
and load your boot with the seeded grapes.*

British English interpretation:

*Before you have an **affair** (walk out) with him latch the **hood of your car** (secure your bonnet) and fill your **car trunk** (boot) with the grapes **with seeds** (seeded).*

North American English interpretation:

*Before you **leave** (walk out) with him fasten your **head covering** (bonnet) and fill your **footwear** (boot) with the **seedless** (Seeded) grapes.*

In the above illustration, the sentence is in the English Language yet the comprehension of the sentence is completely different due to the culture, context and concepts being understood.

As you can see, language is complex and marvelous whether it is spoken, written, sung or signed. Sign language is equally complex and wonderful to those who understand it.

If there already is an established sign language where you will be ministering, **learn their signs**. DO NOT try to impose your American Sign Language on them.

One great error we make is to criticize the sign language of another country because it looks silly or has no basis in our logic. Thus you say, "My sign is better than yours. Mine is a smarter sign." On what would you base that type of reasoning? Their sign language makes perfect sense to them and has a basis in THEIR logic and in the way they conceptualize and think. Who are we to judge whose "logic" is right when it comes to signs and concepts?

Deaf are very sensitive in this area. They are fiercely nationalistic when it comes to their language. By the way, you are equally sensitive to this as well. You would not accept some foreigner coming and criticizing your language or trying to change it.

The countries that you serve in may not have an advanced sign language. If this is the case, try to use what signs that you find the Deaf using and then help them build upon them using their language as the foundation for a formal sign language.

Many may have a basic sign language but lack certain technical or Christian signs. It would not be improper to borrow signs from one language to help form another. You do not necessarily need to borrow American signs, but you can consult various other countries that have similar spoken languages or cultural roots to see what their sign for a particular concept is.

An important thing to remember is as the Deaf community grows and becomes more sophisticated, they may wish to develop their own language that may differ from what you have been using. Do not be offended but do your best to be a wise participant in this process.

Countries that have advanced Deaf cultures are very protective of their country and signs. They do not need others coming in and trying to change their language. Missionaries need to adapt to the national culture, not the other way around.

A missionary would never go to a country with an established verbal language and seek to "correct" or change their language to what seems to suit the missionary. That would be arrogant, unethical and wrong. The same can be said for those who would do that with a country's sign language. It is one thing to help develop what does not exist. It is another thing entirely to attempt to change what is already there.

Finally, remember, even within a country there are variations to signs. You may be using one sign in one part of the country and find the Deaf in another part use a completely different sign for the same concept. The signs for *picnic* and *birthday* in American

Sign Language are good examples of this. There are several signs for each of these, depending on where in the country you live.

Finally, once again, <u>learn</u> <u>the</u> <u>language</u> <u>well</u>. Take the time to make an investment that will make a great deal of difference in your ability to minister and in your ability to interact and get along in the country you will be working. You will save a great deal of personal frustration in the course of your ministry and be much better prepared to minister.

The Caceres Family
Manuel, Renzo, Naomi, Paula, and Lisa

The missionary mentioned at the beginning of this chapter, Manuel Caceres, made great strides in learning the Peruvian Sign Language. He and his wife Paola, who is a professional interpreter in the Argentine Sign Language, did not come to Peru and try to change Peruvian Sign Language. On the contrary, they have - used Peruvian Sign Language to help augment their own with the Christian and religious signs that they did not have in Argentina.

This author would dare say that the Ephraimites had wished they had learned the Gileadites language well!

Because of their lack of skill in the language of the Gileadites, 42,000 Ephraimites were killed. The Gileadites defeated the Ephraimites and captured the fords of the Jordan. (Judges 12:4-5)

From *The Brick New Testament*
http://www.thebricktestament.com/judges/42000_ephraim-ites_killed/jg12_04-05.html

SIGN LANGUAGE AROUND THE WORLD

Therefore is the name of it called Babel; because the LORD did there confound the language of all the earth: and from thence did the LORD scatter them abroad upon the face of all the earth.

- Genesis 11:9

In April of 1987, one of the largest warships in the world made a port call in Toulon, France. The Aircraft Carrier, USS Nimitz, was an imposing figure in this French port city. She was quietly tucked into the harbor of this major French Navy town.

A young Christian Sailor who was on deployment on board Nimitz had the opportunity to visit a small French Baptist Church. There he met a family where the mother and father were Deaf.

This sailor was involved in the Deaf ministry at his home church back in Jacksonville, Florida and was excited to meet deaf people from another country. He had the opportunity to do something for this family that they never thought would be possible. He was able to give them a tour of the Nimitz and explain its workings for them.

Though the languages were different, there were many similarities and basic communication took place across the world, across cultures and across languages. The sailor left an American Sign Language book and several illustrative Chick tracts with the family. This had a great impact on that young sailor. Today he is a missionary to the Deaf in Peru, South America and the author of this book.

As stated before; sign language is not universal. In every country and even within countries, there are different sign languages or signing systems and dialects used.

There is an International Sign Language sometimes used by the Deaf during international forums and sporting events. In 1973 the *Commission of Unification of Signs* a committee of the *World Federation of the Deaf,* produced the first standardized vocabulary. A book was published in the early 1970's titled *Gestuno: International Sign Language of the Deaf.* This book had a vocabulary list of about 1500 signs.

This system relies on the signers own grammatical structure and syntax as well as a heavy use of *Classifiers* which are hand shapes that act as identifiers for objects, mime and gestures to bridge the language barrier. You can read more about International Sign Language at *http://en.wikipedia.org/wiki/Gestuno.*

Language is a very nationalistic issue, which is deeply rooted in the cultural heritage of any people; especially for deaf people. According to a *New York Times* article dated Sunday, October 24, 1999 by Lawrence Osborne entitled *A Linguistic Big Bang;* there are over 200 different official sign languages around the world being used by Deaf and hard-of-hearing people.

This article chronicles the unique and exceptional development of Nicaraguan Sign Language by deaf children. These children developed their own sign language with all of its grammar, syntax and expressions. This has been a linguist's dream to study, as it was the development of a language out of basically nothing more than a need.

More and more, sign languages are being recognized in countries all around the world as official languages. Deaf are claiming their cultural and linguistic heritage as they are gaining respect and recognition in their home countries.

In many countries, their sign language was developed in part by American missionaries or workers who went to that country and found that there was no official sign language. Because of this, these missionaries and workers "borrowed" many American Sign

Language signs and concepts and incorporated them into that country's Deaf culture to help them develop their own signing system. Hence, there are many countries that have a sign language very similar to American Sign Language. Some countries like this are, Bolivia, Ecuador, Peru and the Philippines, just to mention a few.

As the Deaf become more educated and enlightened, they become more organized and their sign languages begin to evolve and become more and more distinct. In many countries, there are Deaf associations and clubs that are working to nationalize their languages.

This can be a very frustrating process for some, as the Deaf themselves do not always agree on what signs to use. In addition, in an attempt to nationalize their signs, they reject out of a sense of pride or political affiliation, the signs that they have used over the years that were borrowed from America or another country's sign language. Logic or reason, are often not participants in this endeavor.

In Peru, there was no functioning modern sign language for the Deaf. Each family or small group with deaf members had their own "home signs." These home signs were very limited and basic gestures. When Missionary Vernon Miller arrived in the late 1960's, there was no Peruvian Sign Language to learn. Together with others who had an interest in the Deaf, he helped to develop Peruvian Sign Language and the first official publication was produced through the *Ministry of Education.*

Through *Efata*, Vernon began to train and teach hearing and deaf people this new Peruvian Sign Language. They then began to teach others. Through this influence Peruvian Sign Language became richer.

Some regional differences began to emerge. These differences emerged through different schools, cities and associations for the Deaf where there was little social contact among the groups. These same variations can be seen in any language and people groups.

Beginning in the late 1990's and up until today, the Peruvian Deaf Association has tried unsuccessfully to establish an official Peruvian Sign Language apart from the one that already exists. They have not been able to do so as there is too much in-fighting in the process. Everyone wants their sign to be the "right" one and they wish to reject the signs that have been used for years that were taught by *Efata* because they are "American" signs.

In reality, many of the signs they are rejecting are not American at all. However, because they are used at *"Efata,"* they are labeled as being American because they were developed with the assistance of an American missionary.

Another reason for this rejection is that deaf people are very proud of their culture and language and wish to have their own language. This is a good thing as long as they maintain objectiveness in the process and do not reject years of work and language development because of Deaf or cultural pride.

Some Deaf Associations in Peru do not wish to allow hearing people to be active and effective participants in the process of evolving the development of Peruvian Sign Language. Or at the very least, they wish to diminish this participation. This is due to several reasons. One is this very same Deaf pride. The Deaf will do it! They do not want hearing people to dominate the process. Instead of looking to find a balance of cooperation, they reject the help of the hearing people who could be a very positive and collaborative force in this process.

Unfortunately, this situation has been repeated in many countries. All one can do is try to work together in this area for the common good of the Deaf and their language.

Also, there are people from other countries that for reasons of their own are instigating the anti-American Sign Language movement. They travel to other countries and hold seminars to try to convince the Deaf in those countries to reject the American influence.

This is an unfortunate political bias that at times creeps into the language discourse. What the Deaf fail to realize is that although there may be similarities to another country's sign language, their language is still their own, no matter where it came from.

American Sign Language is a direct descendent of French Sign Language. Should Americans abandon their language and try to develop one that is completely different because it has its formative roots in French Sign Language? Of course not, that would be ludicrous.

American Sign Language evolved into its own language with its own structures and forms that are distinct from French Sign Language. This is natural and occurs in any language. Another country's sign language will do the same. Peruvian Sign Language, though very similar to American Sign Language, continues to evolve, grow and become more distinct just as it should.

Here is another way to look at this language issue. Spanish is a rich and vibrant language. Yet more and more, American words are being added to the Spanish lexicon. Most of these words are the result of technical terms such as Internet, pod cast, file, etc. All languages do some borrowing. The English language, for example, is a mixture of various languages; French, German, Latin, Saxon, etc. There is no shame or diminishing of a nation's culture or language just because there is borrowing that takes place in the language.

Because the Deaf live in a silent world they do not notice when this borrowing takes place in the hearing world around them. Thus, they are more protective of their sign language as their sign language is an integral part of their Deaf culture.

For those who are curious about world sign languages, please refer to the *Appendix at* the end of this book.

FINAL
THOUGHTS

And the things that thou hast heard of me among many witnesses, the same commit thou to faithful men, who shall be able to teach others also.

- 2 Timothy 2:2

As the pastor and his visitation partner approached the wood-frame home on the quiet residential street, the partner was filled with anticipation. This was the first time he had ever gone out with the pastor to visit the Deaf. He was just beginning to learn American Sign Language and had been studying hard.

The young man was in awe of the pastor. He noticed that as he was driving down the road, the pastor would fingerspell many of the words on the signs that they would pass. His fingers were constantly working as his hand rested on the gear shifter. It was all so natural for him.

They approached the door and knocked. No one responded. The partner thought that no one was home. The Pastor knocked again, harder; again, no response. Then, with no thought for his dignity, the pastor began to jump up and down on the wood porch as if it was nothing! Lo, and behold, the door opened, and the visit began. The partner was dumbfounded but thrilled. Thus was his welcome into the ministry of Deaf visitation!

Without a doubt, the greatest limitation that we have in ministry to the Deaf is the lack of trained committed deaf and hearing people who are able to *"teach others also."*

We as Independent Fundamental Baptists must develop a passion for this needed work, for while we are asleep in our comfort zones, the cults are working to ensnare the Deaf into their Hellish organizations. The Jehovah's Witnesses are all over South and Central America; as are the Mormons.

Hence the question: Where shall the Deaf go? *We* have the words of eternal life! We must do all we can to make it available to them.

Pastor, Seek to Meet the Need

There is a great need for outreach among the Deaf. You as the pastor may not know sign language and frankly may not have the time or talent to invest in learning it because you are greatly involved in your ministry. That is understandable. However, there may be someone in your church that you can send to learn sign language and to learn how to minister to the Deaf. **You provide the VISION, and let your people capture it, develop it and make it happen. You do not need to do it all yourself. God gave you a church full of people just waiting to be challenged and trained to serve Him.**

Look for those who may be *"apt"* in the area of Deaf ministry and challenge them in it. If the person is involved in another area of ministry, allow them the opportunity and option to choose Deaf ministry and transfer their current ministry tasks to another. Make it happen. Make a way! Your people will never become passionate about that which you are not passionate. It is much easier to fill a position of need in hearing ministry than in Deaf ministry.

A Deaf ministry **cannot** succeed without the full support of the church Pastor. He is the most vital person in the local church in regards to developing and implementing the vision and mission outreach.

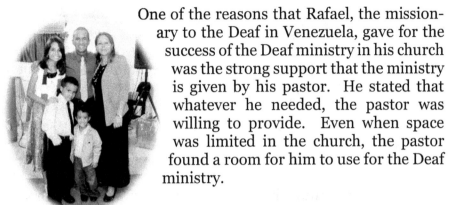

One of the reasons that Rafael, the missionary to the Deaf in Venezuela, gave for the success of the Deaf ministry in his church was the strong support that the ministry is given by his pastor. He stated that whatever he needed, the pastor was willing to provide. Even when space was limited in the church, the pastor found a room for him to use for the Deaf ministry.

The Ramirez Family

Deaf Ministry Is Not Just for Ladies

An unfortunate misconception people have is that Deaf ministry is "women's work." This stems from the observation that most interpreters that people see are women and the fact that it is looked upon as a "nurture" ministry.

Be grateful for every dear sister in Christ who has given their time and talent to work with deaf people. Were it not for each one of them, many Deaf would be burning in Hell today. Thus, in no way should one diminish the need for Godly women with a heart and passion to work with the Deaf. However, as the Marines would say: *We're looking for a few good men!*

Who is going to *preach* to the Deaf? Who is going to challenge and motivate young, Deaf men to become preachers, evangelists, missionaries and Christian men of character and integrity? This requires OTHER MEN, both deaf and hearing. We must rise up and meet the challenge. We must do the job. We must be the role models that will propel the next generation of young men and women, both deaf and hearing, to surrender their lives for the cause of Christ at home and abroad.

Deaf Ministry Does Cost

As in any ministry there are costs. Bus ministries, for example, are very expensive ministries for a church. However, untold thousands have been reached through the bus ministry. Even some of our well-known pastors were reached through this ministry. How many men and women today have a secure place in eternity because someone cared to pick them up and bring them to church on church buses or vans?

During the high days of the bus ministry, churches would spare no expense in picking up those children and families who would come. Few ever said, "If those children and poor families do not tithe, we will no longer pick them up." "They are just too costly and 'high maintenance' to continue serving them." "They don't pay their fair share or carry their load."

Yet, this has been the attitude for years concerning Deaf ministry. Churches will pay salaries and benefits for a children's pastor, youth pastor, co-pastor, seniors' pastor, visitation pastor, outreach pastor, connections pastor or bus pastor. However, try to hire a full or even part-time pastor to the Deaf and some will say, "Why, we cannot afford that." Or, "Well, we need a janitor for the church. We can hire a janitor who can double as the Deaf pastor."

In addition to the staff needs and expenses, there are also transportation needs. Many Deaf require transportation to come to church. Without it, they would never be able to come. As well, there are the normal ministry costs for materials and facilities specifically geared to Deaf ministry.

Ministry = service = sacrifice = giving

That is the basic formula. It is the formula for hearing ministry as well as Deaf ministry. Ministry COSTS!

One of the greatest costs of Deaf ministry is not the cost in dollars, but the cost in time. There is a large investment in time required to have an effective and growing Deaf ministry. Deaf people generally need more assistance in social, medical and legal areas than hearing people, mainly due to their inability to hear. They need interpreters, facilitators and counselors for things that are personal, social and family related that may not have anything to do with Bible teaching or ministry.

One must remember that when we help in these areas, we are helping the whole person, which builds confidence and relationships. Through these relationships, we build trust and gain access to share the Gospel, disciple and strengthen the spiritual lives of deaf people.

Deaf Ministries Need Your Best and Brightest

God uses people in many areas of ministry. Many times the Deaf ministry is the repository for those who have been deemed unable to minister with "regular" people.

The Deaf notice when a hearing person is placed in the Deaf ministry because they do not "fit" anywhere else. If a person cannot minister to hearing people due to emotional or other personal issues, why does one think that they will be effective in Deaf ministry where the challenges are much greater?

The Deaf may not be able to hear, but they can see. They are not stupid. In fact, they are at times more perceptive of motivations and actions than hearing people. Thus, they are more sensitive to these types of issues. When we do not treat the Deaf as equals, this causes great harm in our ability to reach them for Christ. We must do all we can to facilitate ministry to them in the most effective manner.

Comments have been made such as this – "Why would you want to waste your time and talent on the Deaf? You could go far in a hearing ministry." The answer to this is – "Why would one NOT want to spend their life reaching the Deaf for Christ? Jesus seemed to care enough to go out of His way to reach the Deaf (Mark chapter 7). Why would one not consider it an honor to do the same?"

Workers in hearing ministry are plentiful in proportion to those who dedicate their lives to working with the Deaf in full-time ministry. A faithful, dedicated and apt Deaf worker, *"Who can find"*!

There is no "wasted talent" in the Lord's work. For example, a young Bible College student studying to be a full-time missionary or pastor to the Deaf said that he really enjoys music ministry. He has a good voice and likes to sing. The response to him was "Wonderful, the Deaf need some talented people in music to help them get the most out of music that they can."

Scott Crabtree is a missionary to the Deaf. His wife, Tricia, has a very beautiful voice and has a great talent for writing music. She is the author of such songs as *"Bury My heart on the Mission Field"* and *"You're Never Alone."*

Bro. Scott is hard-of-hearing and is not able to appreciate Tricia's beautiful voice as much as hearing people. However, what a great treasure in ministry she is for the Deaf as she works faithfully by his side teaching and training deaf and hearing leaders and workers with the Deaf.

It has been said about some hearing preachers to the Deaf – "Wow, he is a great preacher. Why doesn't he preach to the hearing instead of wasting his abilities on Deaf ministry?" So what you mean is, the Deaf do not need or deserve great preaching?

A Challenge to Be Met

As stated before, working with the Deaf has its own set of challenges and hurdles to overcome. It is a unique sub-culture that has a very distinct flavor and life. It is a rich sub-culture that needs to be reached for the Lord. It can be done, and done successfully, no matter where or in what country one works.

In 2004, a young missionary family that just completed language school agreed to come and fill-in at *Efata* while this author and his family were away. They had very little knowledge of sign language and no knowledge of Deaf culture.

During the month or so that they were in *Efata* before the author left, this author shared with them many of the differences related to working with the Deaf and helped them to begin to learn sign language. During the time while this author and his family were on furlough, many phone calls were made and e-mails exchanged as they shared their frustrations and challenges with the Deaf. This was all so new to them.

Through much prayer and encouragement, they stayed with it and this author was able to return to a vibrant growing ministry. This was a great testimony for this young missionary family and the leadership team of *Efata*.

Later, while talking with him, and sharing with him concerning the writing of this book, he stated that he wished that he had had a book like this before he began working at *Efata*. This author told him, "You probably would not have come!"

He said that the culture shock that he experienced in ministering to the Deaf was <u>far greater</u> that the culture shock of moving to Peru, learning the Spanish language and adjusting to Peruvian culture and life. He said that it was by far the <u>most difficult time</u> he has ever had in learning and adjusting to another culture.

Deaf ministry IS a challenge and a sub-culture that is very difficult to understand and assimilate. Its complexities go beyond manner of dress, food preferences and social norms. It is in essence a completely foreign way of thinking, communicating and living, no matter where you go in the world. It is an emotional, intellectual and spiritual difference that must be bridged in order for effective long-lasting ministry to take place among the Deaf.

Is it a challenge? Yes; however, as Paul challenged Timothy:

> *I charge thee therefore before God, and the Lord Jesus Christ, who shall judge the quick and the dead at his appearing and his kingdom; Preach the word; be instant in season, out of season; reprove, rebuke, exhort with all longsuffering and doctrine.* - 2 Timothy 4:1-2

Just Do It

In 1986, this author went to his first national Deaf conference in Peoria, Illinois. It was the D.B.F.A. – *Deaf Baptist Fellowship of America*.

In that conference he was challenged and motivated to just "DO IT!" The preacher in his message to both Deaf and hearing was fingerspelling the words with both hands and "throwing them" out to the audience – Do it! Do it! Do it! It was astounding to see how fast and crisp he was able to do that. This was a direct challenge to DO what God had for this author to do in serving the Lord in Deaf ministry.

That week was a life-changing week where the need for workers and preachers for the Deaf was clearly presented and seen. The attendees were wonderfully challenged and encouraged to press on and not quit. It was also during that week that this author decided that no matter where the Lord sent him or what God has in store for him, he was going to dedicate his life to working with the Deaf in some way. God was moving in this author's life and he was ready to listen.

It appeared however, that quitting was a major problem among Deaf workers. Burnout, frustration and difficulties in ministry seemed to be taking a heavy toll among the workers with the Deaf. Many who were in Deaf ministry back then are no longer there today for a multitude of reasons.

In every conference for the Deaf this author has ever had the privilege to attend or participate in; one of the primary themes has always been: "Don't quit, stay faithful and just do it!"

Paul said at the end of his life and ministry:

I have fought a good fight, I have finished my course, I have kept the faith: - 2 Timothy 4:7

These are words that we should live by. The Deaf world NEEDS this type of dedication in ministry. Thank God for those who are dedicating their lives t this very vital ministry outreach around the world.

We must fight the good fight of faith to reach the Deaf with the Gospel of the Lord Jesus Christ before it is too late.

Pastor, church member, missionary, Christians all, we have a job to do, a valuable and Christ-honoring ministry of outreach that brings great joy in Heaven over Deaf sinners who repent and trust Christ as Savior. **REMEMBER:**

*"How then shall they call on him in whom they have not believed? and how shall they believe in him **of whom they have not heard**? and **how shall they hear without a preacher**? And how shall they preach, except they be sent..."*
— Romans 10:14-15

In all Christian endeavors we need to stay the course and continue the work. We have plenty of "dutiful" Christians. In Luke chapter 17 the Bible says in verse 10, *"So likewise ye, when ye shall have done all those things which are commanded you, say, We are unprofitable servants: we have done that which was our duty to do."*

It is time that we produce more "Medal of Honor" Deaf workers. We have plenty who *"are unprofitable servants: we have done that which was our duty to do."*

Doing our "duty" is NOT enough in these last days and times. We must go ABOVE AND BEYOND our duty. We MUST rise above the norm, the mediocrity of everyday Christianity and begin to *"Fight the good fight of faith"* in Deaf ministry. **_LET'S JUST DO IT!_**

Appendix

This information was obtained from the Gallaudet University Library website at *http://library.gallaudet.edu/dr/faq-world-sl-country.html.*

Sign Languages of the World, By Country

Derived from the Ethnologue database (www.ethnologue.com/, 11/8/01, "SEARCH THE WEB VERSION" link), with many additional sign languages, categorization, and much other information added by Thomas R. Harrington. Known now-extinct sign languages are indicated by "(defunct)."

Sign languages are divided into three categories:

DEAF SIGN LANGUAGES are the natural languages developed by Deaf people and used in everyday life. In many countries, the Deaf sign languages are barred in schools for the deaf and are used mainly outside the classroom and within the Deaf community. Often, particularly in developing countries, non-native Deaf sign languages have been introduced by religious missionaries and by educators of the Deaf who were trained in other countries. This explains the apparent oddity of finding, as just one example out of many, Norwegian Sign Language used by some Deaf people in Madagascar. Numerous other countries have had more than one foreign sign language imported. In many countries, in the absence of a unifying national institution or agency for the Deaf, different regional sign language dialects have developed in the areas around different schools for the Deaf.

CODE SYSTEMS attempt to represent a spoken language in manual form, and are usually invented by hearing people, often borrowing signs from the local Deaf sign language but in the word order of, and following the grammar and syntax of, the spoken language. These systems are used for pedagogical purposes in the schools, and only rarely by Deaf people outside the classroom. This category also includes the pidgins, or contact languages, which arise when Deaf and hearing people attempt to communicate with each other. Pidgins commonly use signs from the local Deaf sign language, but use them in the spoken language's word order and omit both the spoken language's and Deaf language's details of grammar and syntax. Cued Speech, a system of manual signals to supplement speechreading, and the similar Danish Mouth-Hand System are also included in this Code Systems category. So is the Rochester Method, which consists of fingerspelling everything in spoken English.

ALTERNATIVE SIGN LANGUAGES are non-Deaf sign languages, developed and used primarily by some groups of hearing people for various special purposes when speaking is not possible or not permitted, though those languages may also be used by Deaf members of that particular group.

Algeria
DEAF SIGN LANGUAGE:
Algerian Sign Language

American Samoa
DEAF SIGN LANGUAGE:
American Sign Language

Argentina
DEAF SIGN LANGUAGE:
Argentine Sign Language
DIALECT:
Córdoba Sign Language

Armenia
DEAF SIGN LANGUAGE:
Armenian Sign Language
ALTERNATIVE SIGN LANGUAGE:
Armenian Women's Sign Language = Caucasian Sign Language (defunct)

Australia
DEAF SIGN LANGUAGE:
Australian Sign Language (derived from British Sign Language, with influences from American Sign Language and Irish Sign Language.)
"Australasian Sign Language" is an attempt to merge Australian Sign Language and New Zealand Sign Language into one common sign language.
CODE SYSTEM:
Cued Speech (especially in Catholic schools for the deaf)
ALTERNATIVE SIGN LANGUAGES:
Australian Aborigines Sign Language
DIALECTS:
Aranda (or Arunta) Sign Language
Dieri Sign Language
Djingili Sign Language
Jaralde Sign Language
Manjiljarra Sign Language
Mudbura Sign Language
Murngin Sign Language
Ngada Sign Language
Torres Straits Islander Sign Language
Walpiri [or Walbiri] Sign Language
Warumungu [or Warramunga] Sign Language

Western Desert Sign Language (Yurira Watjalku)
Worora Kinship Sign Language

Austria
DEAF SIGN LANGUAGE:
Austrian Sign Language (related to both French Sign Language and Russian Sign Language)

Bangladesh
DEAF SIGN LANGUAGE:
Bengali Sign Language
Indian Sign Language

Belgium
DEAF SIGN LANGUAGE:
Belgian Sign Language
DIALECTS:
North Belgian Sign Language
South Belgian Sign Language
CODE SYSTEMS:
Van Beek (Signed Dutch/Flemish, Vlamisch met Gebaren)
Signed French (le Français Signé)

Bolivia
DEAF SIGN LANGUAGE:
Bolivian Sign Language (based on American Sign Language, modified for Spanish spelling)

Botswana
DEAF SIGN LANGUAGES:
American Sign Language
Danish Sign Language
German Sign Language

Brazil
DEAF SIGN LANGUAGES:
Brazilian Sign Language (Língua Brasileira de Sinais, Linguagem das Mãos)
DIALECT:
São Paulo Sign Language
Urubú-Kaapor Sign Language = Urubú Sign Language
Isolated Brazilian Indian tribes are also reported to have their own sign languages.

Bulgaria
DEAF SIGN LANGUAGES:
Bulgarian Sign Language
Russian Sign Language

Burkina Faso
DEAF SIGN LANGUAGE:
American Sign Language

Burundi
DEAF SIGN LANGUAGE:
American Sign Language

Canada
DEAF SIGN LANGUAGES:
American Sign Language
French Canadian Sign Language = Québéc Sign Language (Langue des Signes Québécois)
Sex differences exist due to segregated-sex schools.
Eskimo Sign Language
Nova Scotian Sign Language = Maritime Sign Language
CODE SYSTEMS:
Pidgin Sign English
Signed English
Pidgin Sign French
Signed French
ALTERNATIVE SIGN LANGUAGE:
Sawmill Sign Language (British Columbia)

Chad
DEAF SIGN LANGUAGE:
Chadian Sign Language (derived from American Sign Language via Nigerian Sign Language)

Chile
DEAF SIGN LANGUAGE:
Chilean Sign Language

China (People's Republic)
DEAF SIGN LANGUAGES:
Chinese Sign Language
DIALECT:
Shanghai Sign Language
Other dialects exist.

Hong Kong Sign Language
Macao Sign Language

China (Taiwan)
DEAF SIGN LANGUAGES:
Taiwanese Sign Language (Ziran Shouyu)
DIALECTS:
Taipei
Tainan
[Mainland] Chinese Sign Language
CODE SYSTEM:
Signed Mandarin (Wenfa Shouyu)

Colombia
DEAF SIGN LANGUAGES:
Colombian Sign Language (Lenguaje manual Colombiáno)
Providencia Sign Language

Costa Rica
DEAF SIGN LANGUAGE:
Costa Rican Sign Language

Cuba
DEAF SIGN LANGUAGE:
Cuban Sign Language (Lengua de Señas Cubanas)

Czech Republic
DEAF SIGN LANGUAGE:
Czech Sign Language

Denmark
DEAF SIGN LANGUAGES:
Danish Sign Language
Scandinavian Pidgin Sign Language
CODE SYSTEMS:
Mouth-Hand System
Signed Danish

Dominican Republic
DEAF SIGN LANGUAGE:
Dominican Sign Language

Ecuador
DEAF SIGN LANGUAGE:
Ecuadorian Sign Language

Egypt

DEAF SIGN LANGUAGE:
Egyptian Sign Language

El Salvador
DEAF SIGN LANGUAGE:
El Salvadoran Sign Language

Estonia
DEAF SIGN LANGUAGE:
Estonian Sign Language

Ethiopia
DEAF SIGN LANGUAGE:
Ethiopian Sign Language
Different signs are used in different regional schools for the deaf.
American Sign Language
Finnish Sign Language
Swedish Sign Language

Europe (in general)
ALTERNATIVE SIGN LANGUAGES:
Augustinian Sign Language = Canons Sign Language (defunct)
Benedictine Sign Language
Cistercian Sign Language
Trappist Sign Language

Fiji
DEAF SIGN LANGUAGE:
Fiji Sign Language

Finland
DEAF SIGN LANGUAGES:
Finnish Sign Language (Viittomakieli)
DIALECTS:
 Finnish-language school dialect (17 schools)
 Swedish-language school dialect (1 school)
Scandinavian Pidgin Sign Language
CODE SYSTEMS:
Signed Finnish
Signed Swedish

France
DEAF SIGN LANGUAGES:
French Sign Language (Langue des Signes Française)
DIALECTS:

 Marseilles Sign Language = Southern French Sign Language
Lyons Sign Language
Old French Sign Language (defunct)
CODE SYSTEM:
Signed French (le Français Signé)
ALTERNATIVE SIGN LANGUAGES:
Augustinian Sign Language = Canons Sign Language (defunct)
DIALECTS:
 Paris (defunct)
Benedictine Sign Language
Cistercian Sign Language (Cluny dialect)
Trappist Sign Language

Germany
DEAF SIGN LANGUAGES:
German Sign Language (Deutsche Gebärdensprache)
Many regional lexical variations in western Germany.
Eastern Germany has some different sign languages, a legacy from the Communist days.
CODE SYSTEMS:
Signed German
Speech-Accompanied Signs (Lautbegleitende Gebärden)
Phonemic Manual System (Phonembestimmes Manualsystem)

Ghana
DEAF SIGN LANGUAGES:
Ghanian Sign Language (descended from American Sign Language)
Adamorobe Sign Language
American Sign Language

Great Britain
DEAF SIGN LANGUAGES:
British Sign Language
DIALECT:
 Welsh Sign Language
Old Kentish Sign Language (defunct)
CODE SYSTEMS:
Manually Coded English
Paget-Gorman Sign System
Sign Supported English (SSE)
ALTERNATIVE SIGN LANGUAGES:

Anglo-Saxon Monastic Sign Language (defunct)
Augustinian Sign Language = Canons Sign Language (defunct)
DIALECTS:
 Dublin Cathedral (defunct)
 Ely Cathedral (defunct)
Benedictine Sign Language
Trappist Sign Language

Greece
DEAF SIGN LANGUAGE:
Greek Sign Language

Guatemala
DEAF SIGN LANGUAGE:
Guatemalan Sign Language

Guinea
DEAF SIGN LANGUAGES:
American Sign Language
Guinean Sign Language

Hong Kong, see China (People's Republic)

Guyana
DEAF SIGN LANGUAGE:
Guyana Sign Language (derived from American Sign Language)

Hungary
DEAF SIGN LANGUAGE:
Hungarian Sign Language

Iceland
DEAF SIGN LANGUAGE:
Icelandic Sign Language (evolved from Danish Sign Language)

India
DEAF SIGN LANGUAGE:
Indian Sign Language
DIALECTS:
 Bangalore-Madras Sign Language
 Bombay Sign Language
 Calcutta Sign Language
 Indo-Pakistan Sign Language
 DIALECTS:

 Delhi Sign Language
 North West Frontier Sign Language
 Punjab/Sindh Sign Language
Indian Sign Language and Pakistan Sign Language, and their respective dialects, have traditionally been considered separate sign languages, but recent research indicates that they are actually both dialects of a broader-based Indo-Pakistan Sign Language. More research is needed to determine the relationship among other Indian and Pakistani regional and dialectal sign languages.
ALTERNATIVE SIGN LANGUAGE:
Hindu Dance Gesture Language

Indonesia
DEAF SIGN LANGUAGES:
Indonesian Sign Language (based on Malaysian Sign Language)
Bali Sign Language (Kata Kolok)

International
DEAF SIGN LANGUAGE:
International Sign Language = Gestuno
ALTERNATIVE SIGN LANGUAGES:
Paleno
Worldsign

Iran
DEAF SIGN LANGUAGE:
Persian Sign Language

Ireland
DEAF SIGN LANGUAGE:
[Irish] Deaf Sign Language
CODE SYSTEMS:
Irish Sign Language
Old Irish Sign Language = Cabra Schools Sign Language
Traditionally in male and female dialects, almost mutually unintelligible, due to strictly sex-segregated education. The two dialects are gradually being merged into one uniform national manual-English version, called Irish Sign Language.

Israel
DEAF SIGN LANGUAGES:

Israeli Sign Language
Minor dialects exist.
Yiddish Sign Language

Italy
DEAF SIGN LANGUAGE:
Italian Sign Language (Lingua Italiana dei Se-
gni or Lingua dei Segni Italiana)
DIALECTS:
Bologna Sign Language
Florence Sign Language
Genova Sign Language
Milan Sign Language
Naples/Palermo Sign Language
Padua Sign Language
Rome Sign Language
Siena Sign Language
Trieste Sign Language
Turin Sign Language

Jamaica
DEAF SIGN LANGUAGES:
Jamaica Country Sign Language
This Sign Language differs considerably from
region to region. No standardized national
Sign Language.
American Sign Language

Japan
DEAF SIGN LANGUAGE:
Japanese Sign Language (Shuwa or Temane
or Nihon Syuwa)
CODE SYSTEMS:
Manually Coded Japanese = Signed Japanese
= Simultaneous Methodic Signs
Pidgin Sign Japanese = Middle Type Signs

Jordan
DEAF SIGN LANGUAGE:
Jordanian Sign Language

Kenya
DEAF SIGN LANGUAGES:
Kenyan Sign Language
Belgian Sign Language (in one school only)
British Sign Language (in one school only)
American Sign Language

Korea (South)
DEAF SIGN LANGUAGE:
Korean Sign Language

Kuwait
DEAF SIGN LANGUAGE:
Kuwaiti Sign Language

Laos
DEAF SIGN LANGUAGE:
Laos Sign Language

Latvia
DEAF SIGN LANGUAGE:
Latvian Sign Language

Libya
DEAF SIGN LANGUAGE:
Libyan Sign Language

Lithuania
DEAF SIGN LANGUAGE:
Lithuanian Sign Language

Macao, see China (People's Republic)

Madagascar (Malagasy Republic)
DEAF SIGN LANGUAGES:
American Sign Language
Norwegian Sign Language

Malaysia (Peninsular)
DEAF SIGN LANGUAGES:
Kuala Lumpur Sign Language (descended
from American Sign Language)
Penang Sign Language
Chinese Sign Language
CODE SYSTEM:
Malaysian Sign Language (Bahasa Malaysia
Kod Tangan, created by the government since
1978; heavily influenced by American Sign
Language)

Mali
DEAF SIGN LANGUAGES:
American Sign Language
Bamako Sign Language

Used in one school for the deaf; uncertain whether it is used in the deaf community outside the school.
French Sign Language
French Canadian Sign Language

Malta
DEAF SIGN LANGUAGE:
Maltese Sign Language (Lingwi tas-Sinjali Maltin)

Mexico
DEAF SIGN LANGUAGES:
Mexican Sign Language (Lenguaje de Señas Mexicanas)
DIALECT:
Ixtapalapa DF Sign Language
Mayan Sign Language = Nohya Sign Language = Yucatec Maya Sign Language (Lenguaje Mímico Maya)

Mongolia
DEAF SIGN LANGUAGE:
Mongolian Sign Language

Morocco
DEAF SIGN LANGUAGES:
Moroccan Sign Language (developed by the Peace Corps from local and American signs)
Algerian Sign Language (in town of Oujda)

Mozambique
DEAF SIGN LANGUAGE:
Mozambican Sign Language

Namibia
DEAF SIGN LANGUAGE:
Namibian Sign Language

Nepal
DEAF SIGN LANGUAGE:
Nepalese Sign Language (developed by the Peace Corps from local and American signs)

Netherlands
DEAF SIGN LANGUAGE:
Dutch Sign Language (developed from French Sign Language)

5 regional dialects, each associated with a particular Dutch school for the deaf.
CODE SYSTEM:
Sign Supported Dutch
Van Beek (Signed Dutch, Nederlands met Gebaren)

New Zealand
DEAF SIGN LANGUAGE:
New Zealand Sign Language
"Australasian Sign Language" is an attempt to merge Australian Sign Language and New Zealand Sign Language into one common sign language.

Ncaragua
DEAF SIGN LANGUAGE:
Nicaraguan Sign Language (Idioma de Signos Nicaragüense)
CODE SYSTEM:
Lenguaje de Signos Nicaragüense (Although this term translates as "Nicaraguan Sign Language", it is in fact a hearing educator-invented code system created for pedagogical purposes, and is separate from the true Deaf-created Nicaraguan Sign Language, or Idioma de Signos Nicaragüense.)

Nigeria
DEAF SIGN LANGUAGES:
Nigerian Sign Language (derived from American Sign Language with local and Ghanian sign influences)
Hausa Sign Language (Maganar Hannu or Managar Bebaye)
American Sign Language

Norway
DEAF SIGN LANGUAGES:
Norwegian Sign Language (Norsk Tegnspråk)
DIALECTS:
Holmestrand School
Oslo School
Trondheim School
Scandinavian Pidgin Sign Language
CODE SYSTEM:
Signed Norwegian

Ottoman Empire, see Turkey

Pakistan
DEAF SIGN LANGUAGES:
Indo-Pakistan Sign Language
DIALECTS:
Karachi Sign Language
Beluchistan Sign Language
Pakistan Sign Language
Punjab/Sindh Sign Language
Pakistan Sign Language and Indian Sign Language have traditionally been considered separate sign languages, but recent research indicates that they are actually both dialects of a broader-based Indo-Pakistan Sign Language. More research is needed to determine the relationship among other Indian and Pakistani regional and dialectal sign languages.
CODE SYSTEM:
Sign Urdu
Palestine
DEAF SIGN LANGUAGE:
Palestinian Sign Language

Paraguay
DEAF SIGN LANGUAGE
Paraguayan Sign Language (Manual Mimico Paraguayo)

Panama
DEAF SIGN LANGUAGE:
Panamanian Sign Language (Lengua de Señas Panameñas)

Papua New Guinea
DEAF SIGN LANGUAGE:
Enga Sign Language

Peru
DEAF SIGN LANGUAGE:
Peruvian Sign Language

Philippines
DEAF SIGN LANGUAGES:
Philippine Sign Language
American Sign Language (common as a second language among Philippine Deaf people)

Poland
DEAF SIGN LANGUAGE:
Polish Sign Language = School Sign Language
Various regional dialects exist.
CODE SYSTEM:
Polish Finger Language (Migany Jezyk Polski)
DIALECTS:
Seeing Essential Polish
Signing Exact Polish

Portugal
DEAF SIGN LANGUAGE:
Portuguese Sign Language (Lingua Gestual Portuguesa, descended from Swedish Sign Language)
DIALECTS:
Lisbon
Oporto
CODE SYSTEM:
Signed Portuguese

Puerto Rico
DEAF SIGN LANGUAGES:
Puerto Rican Sign Language
American Sign Language
CODE SYSTEMS:
Signed Spanish
Signed English

Romania
DEAF SIGN LANGUAGE:
Romanian Sign Language

Russia
DEAF SIGN LANGUAGE:
Russian Sign Language (developed from Austrian Sign Language and French Sign Language with local influence)

Rwanda
DEAF SIGN LANGUAGE:
French Sign Language

Samoa Islands
DEAF SIGN LANGUAGE:

Samoan Sign Language (totally different from the American Sign Language used in neighboring American Samoa)

Saudi Arabia
DEAF SIGN LANGUAGE:
Saudi Arabian Sign Language

Singapore
DEAF SIGN LANGUAGES:
Singapore Sign Language (developed from Shanghai Sign Language and American Sign Language plus local signs)
Shanghai Sign Language
CODE SYSTEM:
Signing Exact English (SEE II)

Slovakia
DEAF SIGN LANGUAGE:
Slovakian Sign Language

Slovenia
DEAF SIGN LANGUAGES:
Slovenian Sign Language (actually a dialect of Yugoslavian Sign Language)
Yugoslavian Sign Language

Solomon Islands: Rennell Island
DEAF SIGN LANGUAGE:
Rennellese Sign Language

South Africa
DEAF SIGN LANGUAGES:
South African Sign Language (descended from British Sign Language)
DIALECTS:
South African Indian Sign Language (Lenasia School)
Other school-based dialects exist.
British Sign Language
Irish Sign Language
American Sign Language
CODE SYSTEM:
Signed Afrikaans
Spain
DEAF SIGN LANGUAGES:

Spanish Sign Language (Lenguaje Gestual Español or Lenguaje Mímico Español or Mímico Español)
Catalonian Sign Language

Sri Lanka
DEAF SIGN LANGUAGES:
Sri Lankan Sign Language
Different deaf schools use different sign languages.\

Swaziland
DEAF SIGN LANGUAGE:
British Sign Language

Sweden
DEAF SIGN LANGUAGES:
Swedish Sign Language
Scandinavian Pidgin Sign Language
CODE SYSTEM:
Signed Swedish

Switzerland
DEAF SIGN LANGUAGES:
Swiss-German Sign Language (Gebärdensprache or Natürliche Gebärde)
DIALECTS:
Bern Sign Language
Zurich Sign Language
Swiss-French Sign Language (Langue des Signes or Langage Gestuelle)
DIALECTS:
Geneva Sign Language
Neuchatel Sign Language
French Sign Language
Swiss-Italian Sign Language
CODE SYSTEM:
Signed German
Speech-Supported Signs (Lautsprachbegleitendes Gebärden)

Taiwan, see China (Taiwan)

Tanzania
DEAF SIGN LANGUAGES:
Tanzanian Sign Language
American Sign Language
Danish Sign Language

Finnish Sign Language
German Sign Language
Swedish Sign Language

Thailand
DEAF SIGN LANGUAGES:
Thai Sign Language (heavily influenced by American Sign Language)
DIALECTS:
Chiangmai Sign Language
Tak Sign Language
Ban Khor Sign Language
Original Chiangmai Sign Language (<1951, defunct)
Original Bangkok Sign Language (<1951, defunct)
At least 5 ethnic groups in mountain regions are also reported to have their own sign languages.

Togo
DEAF SIGN LANGUAGES:
American Sign Language
French Sign Language

Tunisia
DEAF SIGN LANGUAGE:
Tunisian Sign Language

Turkey / Ottoman Empire
DEAF SIGN LANGUAGE:
Turkish Sign Language (Isaret)
Seraglio Sign Language = Harem Sign Language (defunct) (Isaret or Ixarette)

Uganda
DEAF SIGN LANGUAGES:
Ugandan Sign Language (in 1988, several local sign languages were merged into one)
American Sign Language
British Sign Language

Ukraine
DEAF SIGN LANGUAGE:
Ukrainian Sign Language

United Kingdom, see Great Britain

United States of America (also see Puerto Rico)
DEAF SIGN LANGUAGES:
American Sign Language
DIALECT:
Black American Sign Language = Black Southern Sign Language
Hawaii Pidgin Sign Language
Puerto Rican Sign Language
Martha's Vineyard Sign Language (defunct, descended from Old Kentish Sign Language)
CODE SYSTEMS:
Cued Speech
Linguistics of Visual English (LOVE)
Morphemic Sign System
Pidgin Sign English = Conceptually Accurate Signed English (CASE)
Rochester Method
Seeing Essential English (SEE I)
Signed English
Signing Exact English (SEE II)
ALTERNATIVE SIGN LANGUAGES:
Benedictine Sign Language
Cistercian Sign Language (St. Joseph dialect)
Gang Sign Language
Most gang signs are just a few isolated gestures, identifying particular gangs or expressing an attitude or opinion, therefore do not qualify as languages. However, there are reports that in a certain few locations, entire bodies of signs have been developed that are complete enough and expressive enough to carry on a full two-way conversation on various different topics. Those may be regarded as alternative sign languages.
DIALECTS:
El Paso Gang Sign Language
Keresan Pueblo Indian Sign Language
Motorcycle Sign Language
Plains Indians Sign Language
Sawmill Sign Language (Oregon, Washington)
Trappist Sign Language
Underwater Sign Language = Scuba Sign Language (developed by scuba divers, based on American Sign Language)
Uruguay
DEAF SIGN LANGUAGE:
Uruguayan Sign Language

DIALECTS:
Montevideo Sign Language
Salto Sign Language

Venezuela
DEAF SIGN LANGUAGE:
Venezuelan Sign Language

Vietnam
DEAF SIGN LANGUAGES:
Haiphong Sign Language
Hanoi Sign Language
Ho Chi Minh City Sign Language = Saigon
Sign Language
In the past, French Sign Language was used
by missionary teachers in some schools for the
deaf.

Yugoslavia
DEAF SIGN LANGUAGES:
Yugoslavian Sign Language (descended from
Austrian Sign Language and Hungarian Sign
Language)
DIALECT:
Serbian Sign Language
Slovenian Sign Language

Zaïre
DEAF SIGN LANGUAGES:
Congolese Sign Language
French Sign Language

Zambia
DEAF SIGN LANGUAGES:
Zambian Sign Language
American Sign Language

Zimbabwe
DEAF SIGN LANGUAGE:
Zimbabwe Sign Language (Zimsign)
DIALECTS:
Zimbabwe School Sign Language
Masvingo School Sign Language
Zimbabwe Community Sign Language
* * * * * * * * * *

Prepared by Tom Harrington
Reference and Instruction Librarian
February, 2004

RECOMMENDED RESOURCES

Silent Word Ministries
PO Box 889,
Trenton, GA 30752
706-657-8000
www.silentwordministries.org
(This is a highly recommended website with a tremendous amount of resources, information and assistance for Deaf ministry including *Silent Word Ministries International* – the Global missions focus of *Silent Word Ministries.*)

Efata Ministries
Apartado 18-1280
Lima 18, Peru
South América
www.efata.org
(This is the website of the author's ministry in Lima, Peru)

A Basic Course in American Sign Language
T.J. Publishers Inc.
2544 Tarpley Road,
Suite 108
Carrollton, TX 75006
1-800-999-1168
www.tjpublishers.com
(This is the author's recommended sign language course for American Sign Language.)

Deaf Workers' Handbook
By Maxine Jeffries
First Baptist Church, Hammond, Indiana
Copyright 1987
Revised 1991
(This is a practical "how-to" Deaf workers' manual)

Church Planting Village.net
http://www.churchplantingvillage.net/site/c.iiJTKZPE-JpH/b.991689/k.6581/Deaf_in_the_United_States.htm
(This is the church planting information website of the *Southern Baptist Convention's North American Mission Board.* This site has some excellent information and resource lists regarding deafness, Deaf culture and establishing a Deaf ministry in the USA.)

AMERICAN SIGN LANGUAGE ALPHABET

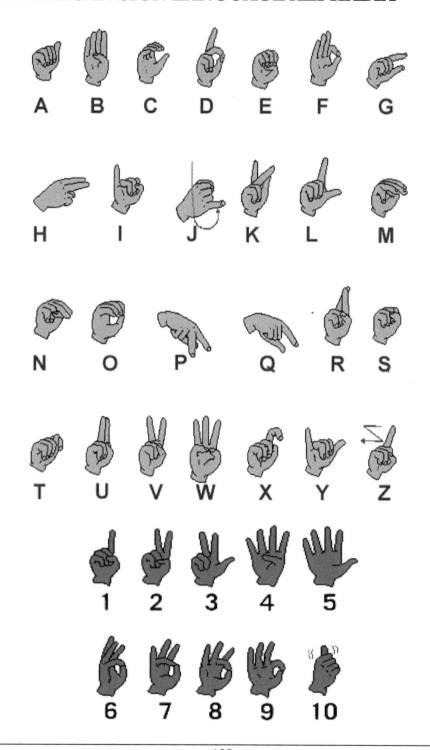

Printed in the USA
CPSIA information can be obtained
at www.ICGtesting.com
CBHW072304180424
7166CB00012B/229